MICROWAVE COOKING WORLDWIDE

MICROWAVE COOKING WORLDWIDE

SONIA ALLISON

UNWIN

HYMAN

LONDON SYDNEY WELLINGTON

First published in Great Britain by Unwin ® Paperbacks, an imprint of Unwin
Hyman Limited in 1988

UNWIN HYMAN LIMITED
15/17 Broadwick Street
London W1V 1FP

Allen & Unwin Australia Pty Ltd
8 Napier Street, North Sydney, NSW 2060, Australia

Allen & Unwin New Zealand Pty Ltd with Port Nicholson Press
60 Cambridge Terrace, Wellington, New Zealand

British Library Cataloguing in Publication Data
Allison, Sonia
  Microwave cooking worldwide
  1. Food: Dishes prepared using microwave ovens – Recipes
  I. Title
  641.5'882
ISBN 0-04-440246-5

Printed in Great Britain at the University Press, Cambridge

CONTENTS

Acknowledgements   8

Introduction   9

Africa – Gabon   14

Africa – Malawi   15

Africa – Southern   17

Australia   19

Austria and Germany   21

Belgium   23

China   26

China – England   33

Europe – Central and Eastern   35

Europe – North and Central   37

France   39

France – Belgium   44

France – Nouvelle Cuisine   45

France – International   46

Germany   49

Great Britain   50

Great Britain – Scotland   59

Great Britain – Wales   61

Great Britain – International   63

CONTENTS

Greece	65
Greece – Middle East	70
Hong Kong	72
Hungary	73
Hungary – Jewish	75
India	77
Indonesia	82
International	84
Israel	91
Italy	92
Japan	97
Jewish	98
Middle East – Balkans	103
Middle East	104
The Netherlands	106
New Zealand	107
Poland	109
Portugal	111
Romania	112
Russia	114

CONTENTS

Scandinavia   117

● Denmark   120

● Finland   122

● Sweden   123

Spain   127

South Africa   129

South America   131

Switzerland   133

USA   135

USA – Chinese   141

USA – Hawaii   142

USA – Italian   144

USA – Louisiana   146

USA – Tex-Mex   151

West Indies   153

INDEX   155

ACKNOWLEDGEMENTS

The author and publishers would like to thank the following organisations for sponsoring photographs for the book. McDougall's Flour (RHM Foods Limited) facing pages 128 below and 129 below; Old El Paso Information Services facing pages 33 below and 48 above; The Pasta Information Centre facing page 49; Paxo (RHM Food Limited) facing page 128; Sea Fish Industry Authority facing pages 32, and 48 below; The Butter Information Council facing pages 129 above and page 145; Tilda Rice facing page 33 above; Uncle Ben's Rice facing page 144 below; Yeoman Instant Mashed potato facing page 144 above.

In addition they wish to thank Glynis Fowles for photographic research and the artist, Paul Saunders.

INTRODUCTION

Understanding Microwaves
Microwaves, based on radar, have been used in cooking appliances for over 40 years and are a form of electro-magnetic energy consisting of short-length, non-ionising and high frequency radio waves at the top end of the radio band. They are near to infra-red rays but not as powerful.

How Microwaves Work in an Oven
In a microwave oven, microwaves are emitted from a device known as a magnetron, usually situated at the top of the oven and placed to one side. They are transmitted into the oven cavity down a channel known as a waveguide then bounce from side to side like a ball. They then beam on to the food from all directions and cause the liquid within the food itself to vibrate so fast that rapid friction is set up which creates enough heat to cook the food cleanly, rapidly and effectively.

Microwave Distribution
To ensure even cooking, most models are fitted with a concealed stirrer fan situated at the top or base of the oven. This rotates while the oven is switched on and helps to distribute the microwaves. The turntables in some models also assist in making sure the waves reach every part of the food.

Shape of Dishes
Because microwaves are able only to penetrate 1 in (2.5 cm) of the food from top to bottom and side to side, shallow dishes for cooking are recommended unless the recipe states otherwise. Round dishes give the best results, followed by oval. Food in square or oblong

dishes sometimes cooks unevenly at the corners.

How To Arrange Food

To allow the microwaves maximum penetration thick pieces of food should be placed towards the outside of the plate or dish, leaving the centre as empty as possible. For example, 3 potatoes or apples etc should be arranged in a triangle, 4 in a square, 6 to 8 in a ring. Food should *never* be piled up as cooking will be noticeably uneven. Stirring some of the dishes during and at the end of cooking helps to distribute heat but this should take place only where recommended in the recipe.

Standing or Resting Times

To enable heat to transfer itself from the outside edges to the centre and ensure even cooking, some dishes should be left to stand halfway through their cooking cycle and/or at the end. Individual recipes will specify.

Warning

Never switch on an empty oven or the magnetron may be damaged.

Cleaning

Wipe out the oven cavity with a clean damp dishcloth then dry with a tea towel. Alternatively, remove stubborn stains with a nail brush dipped in detergent water then rinse off.

Choice Of Crockery

Crockery chosen should be made of materials through which microwaves can pass directly to the food in the same way as sunlight passes through a window pane. These include all the ranges of plastic microware currently on the market from Anchor Hocking, Thorpac, Lakeland Plastics, Bejam and other leading manufacturers; different types of crockery glass (but not crystal), and glass ceramic cookware such as Corningware and Pyrex; roasting or boiling bags, cling film (also known as plastic wrap) from British Alcan; basketware, paper and wood. Metal containers should NEVER be used as they reflect microwaves away from the food and prevent it from cooking. Similarly, crockery with silver and gold trims should not be used as they can have a damaging effect on the magnetron and also on themselves. Although most utensils remain relatively cool to the touch, some absorb a surprising amount of heat from the food. Thus, to prevent discomfort, dishes should be removed from the microwave with hands protected by oven gloves.

Browning Dish

This is a ceramic dish, its base coated with special tin oxide material. It becomes extremely hot when pre-heated and is useful for searing or 'frying' food prior to cooking. The food browns on the outside and looks as if cooked by conventional grilling or frying. The dish is always pre-heated while empty for about 5 minutes though this varies according to the food being cooked. Be guided by the recipes or instruction book accompanying the browning dish. It is important to note that every time a batch of food has been cooked, the dish will need cleaning and pre-heating for half the length of time required initially. Although the dish yellows while in use, it returns to its old colour when cold.

Temperature Probe

This registers the internal temperature of joints of meat etc. as an indication of whether they are done.

Power Controls

In general, microwave ovens vary between 500 and 700 watt outputs with corresponding inputs of 1000 and 1500 watts. Recipes in this book have been prepared in a Creda Micro-Plus oven with a 600 watt output and the following variable power settings:

600 watts	FULL POWER	(100% power)
500 watts	REHEAT	(83% power)
400 watts	ROAST	(67% power)
325 watts	SIMMER	(54% power)
230 watts	DEFROST	(38% power)
100 watts	WARM	(17% power)

Cooking times have been given for a 600 watt oven.
For a 500 watt oven *increase* timing by approximately 25 seconds for each minute.
For a 700 watt oven *decrease* timing by approximately 25 seconds for each minute.

Note

The quantities for recipes in this book are given in imperial and metric measurements. It is important not to mix these measurements in any given recipe as they are proportionate.

For microwave cooking you are advised to use cling wrap without plasticizers.

AFRICA - GABON

Okra and Cabbage

Serves 6
Power Level Full
Cooking Time 12 minutes

2oz (50g) pine nuts

1lb (240g) green cabbage or spring greens

3oz (75g) onions

7oz (200g) okra (ladies' fingers)

---

2 tblsp groundnut oil

½pt (275ml) boiling water

---

2 level tblsp salt

½ to 4 level tsp cayenne pepper

Food from this part of Africa is generally fiery hot but I have turned down the heat by using considerably less cayenne pepper than usual. If you like food hot hot, use the increased alternative. This is a vegetarian style contribution which is pleasurable with boiled potatoes or rice.

1. Lightly toast pine nuts under the grill.

2. Thoroughly wash cabbage or greens and shred finely. Peel onions and grate. Wash and scrub okra to remove 'fur' from skin, top and tail then cut into chunks.

3. Pour oil into a large bowl. Leave uncovered and heat for 2 minutes. Stir in all prepared vegetables followed by last 3 ingredients. Toss well to mix.

4. Cover with cling wrap, nick twice and cook 7 minutes. Stand 5 minutes then finally cook a further 3 minutes. Stand another 5 minutes, drain if necessary and serve hot.

14

AFRICA-MALAWI

Greens with Vegetables and Peanuts

Serves 4–6
Power Level Full Power
Cooking Time 25 minutes

1lb (450g) green cabbage, spring greens or curly kale
¼pt (150g) boiling water
1 to 2 level tsp salt
8oz (225g) tomatoes
2–3oz (50 to 75g) onions
3oz (75g) peanut butter

Cooked to 'al dente' perfection, this unexpected mix of vegetables and peanut butter blends comfortably with brown rice and the more European pearl barley. A tasty vegetarian stand-by for winter at no great cost.

1. Thoroughly wash cabbage or greens and shred finely, either by hand or in a food processor. Transfer to a large bowl and mix in water and salt.

2. Cover with cling wrap, nick twice and cook 20 minutes. Stand while preparing rest of ingredients.

3. Put tomatoes into a bowl and cover with boiling water. Leave to stand 5 minutes; drain, skin and slice. Peel onions and chop.

4. Uncover cabbage and toss in tomatoes, onions and peanut butter. Cover as above and cook a further 5 minutes.

AFRICA-SOUTHERN

Serves 4 generously
Power Level Full
Cooking Time 20 minutes

8 chicken thighs (2¹/₂lb or 1¹/₄kg)

1¹/₂oz (40g) fresh coconut

1 green chilli

1 garlic clove

6oz (175g) onions

1 level tsp turmeric or 12 saffron strands (the latter is expensive)

1 level tsp ground ginger

1 to 2 level tsp mild curry powder

3 heaped tblsp coarsely chopped fresh coriander leaves

Milk from coconut (about ¹/₄pt or 150ml)

Spiced Chicken with Coconut and Coriander

Exquisitely-flavoured yet only mildly curried, this is a Southern African speciality which is generally eaten with white rice and chutney. If you can use fresh coconut, it makes all the difference to the overall flavour; if not substitute 3 tablespoons dried coconut soaked for half an hour in ¼ pint or 150ml boiling water.

17

1 carton (225g or 8oz) cottage cheese with chives (a substitute for traditional curds)

1. Wash and dry chicken and remove skin. Arrange round edge of a 10-inch (25cm) round dish, squashing pieces together if necessary.

2. Cover with cling wrap, nick twice and cook 10 minutes, turning twice.

3. Cut away brown skin from coconut then grate flesh fairly coarsely into a bowl. De-seed chilli and chop. Peel garlic and crush. Add both to bowl.

4. Peel onions then chop or grate. Add to bowl with turmeric or saffron, ginger, curry, coriander, coconut milk (or dried coconut and water) and finally cottage cheese with chives.

5. Spoon over chicken, cover as above and cook 10 minutes, turning 4 times. Stand 5 minutes.

Note

This dish yields plenty of sauce so make sure you cook adequate supplies of rice. For ease of serving, put chicken and curry into soup plates.

AUSTRALIA

Makes 16
Power Level Full and
Defrost
Cooking Time 11–11½
minutes

8oz (225g) self raising flour

1 level tsp bicarbonate of soda

6oz (175g) soft margarine

6oz (175g) caster sugar

3 eggs (Grade 3)

1 tsp vanilla essence

4 tblsp milk

Chocolate Icing

7oz (200g) plain chocolate

2 level tblsp cocoa powder

8 tblsp warm water

12oz (350g) icing sugar, sifted

Lamingtons

These are cakes which belong strictly to Australia, along with Vegemite which we are at last beginning to import. The cakes are cut into square shapes like dice, dipped in chocolate icing and tossed in coconut. A bit of a bother, but not for those from down under. Despite an assortment of comments to the contrary, cakes DO work in the microwave and this one is an excellent example of success.

1. Line a 9-inch (13cm) square dish with cling wrap, making sure it is as wrinkle-free as possible.

2. Sift flour into a food processor bowl with bicarbonate of soda. Add rest of ingredients and blend until completely smooth.

3. Scrape into lined dish, leave uncovered, and cook 7 minutes at full, turning dish 4 times. Remove from oven and cool to lukewarm. Lift cake and cling wrap on to a wire rack and leave until completely cold before cutting into 16 cubes.

Coating

About 6oz (175g) desiccated coconut

4. For icing, break up chocolate and put into a bowl. Add cocoa and 2 tblsp water. Leave uncovered and heat 4 to 4½ minutes at defrost until chocolate melts.

5. Stir well then work in icing sugar alternately with rest of water to make a moderately soft icing.

6. Coat cubes all over with icing then toss in the coconut.

AUSTRIA AND GERMANY

2oz (50g) fresh white
breadcrumbs

2oz (50g) calf or chicken
liver, minced

2 slightly rounded tsp very
finely chopped parsley

1 level tsp minced dried onion

¼ level tsp marjoram

¼ level tsp salt

Freshly ground black pepper

½ Grade 3 egg, beaten

1¼pt (750ml) clear beef stock

Liver Dumpling Soup

An old pleasure from Austria and Southern
Germany, these little liver dumplings are
companionable in good meat stock, always clear,
and made from beef bones and vegetables.

1. Put crumbs, liver, parsley, onion, marjoram,
   salt, pepper and egg into a bowl. Mix

21

thoroughly and divide into 12 small
dumplings.

2. Pour stock into a fairly deep dish and heat for
10 to 12 minutes or until boiling.

3. Add dumplings to stock and cook 3 to
4 minutes or until they have risen slightly and
floated to the top.

4. Ladle into warm soup bowls and serve
straight away, while still very hot.

BELGIUM

Serves 4–6
Power Level Full
Cooking Time 20 minutes

1 large, round lettuce
3oz (75g) watercress
½ box mustard and cress
4oz (125g) white part of leek
½pt (275ml) boiling water
3 level tblsp cornflour
½pt (275ml) milk
1oz (25g) butter or margarine
1½ to 2 level tsp salt

Vegetable Purée Soup

Reputed to have the best soups in Western Europe, here is a fine example of what Belgian cooking is all about – quality and quantity.

1. Tear off any damaged outer leaves from lettuce, wash well and shake dry. Shred coarsely. Wash watercress and drain. Rinse mustard and cress under cold water and cut off level with top of box. Wash and dry leek then slice.

2. Place all 4 ingredients into a fairly large bowl then add water. Cover with cling wrap and nick twice. Cook 10 minutes, turning 3 times. Stand 5 minutes.

3. Transfer cooked ingredients to a blender goblet and run machine until mixture turns into a fine purée. Return to bowl.

4. Blend cornflour smoothly with milk. Add to

purée with butter or margarine and salt. Leave uncovered and cook 10 minutes. Stand 2 minutes. Stir round, ladle into warm soup plates and serve.

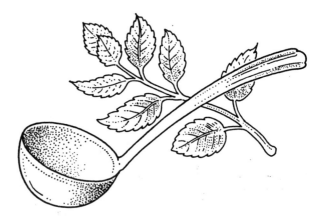

**Serves 4
Power Level Full
Cooking Time 25–25½ minutes**

4 large heads of chicory, each weighing 6 to 7oz (175 to 200g)

¼pt (150ml) boiling water

1 tblsp lemon juice

1½ level tsp salt

Cold milk

4 large slices of ham (8oz or 225g)

1oz (25g) butter or margarine

Ham Wrapped Chicory in Cheese Sauce

One of the joys of Belgian cuisine, chicory with ham in its cocoon of rich cheese sauce makes a fine meal and partners especially well with new potatoes garnished with chopped parsley. To prevent language barriers, the Belgian (or Flemish word) for chicory is witloof and if the Belgian variety is unavailable, substitute neighbouring Dutch which is superb.

1. Wash chicory, taking away any damaged or bruised outer leaves. Remove cores from

1oz (25g) flour
5oz (150g) Emmental cheese, grated
1 level tsp Dijon mustard

bases of each with a potato peeler to reduce bitterness.

2. Place against sides of an 8-inch (20cm) square dish. Add boiling water and lemon juice then sprinkle with salt. Cover with cling wrap, nick twice and cook 12 minutes, turning dish 4 times. Stand 3 minutes.

3. Drain liquid carefully into a measuring cup and make up to ½pt with milk. Wrap ham round chicory and return to dish as before.

4. In separate dish, melt butter or margarine, uncovered, for 1½ to 2 minutes. Stir in flour and cook 1 minute. Gradually whisk in chicory water and milk.

5. Cook, uncovered, for 5 minutes, whisking after every minute. Stir in two-thirds of the cheese and mustard and cook a further 1½ minutes. Stir round and spoon over chicory. Sprinkle with rest of cheese and reheat, uncovered, for 4 minutes. Stand 3 minutes and serve.

CHINA

2 sea bass, each 1lb (450 to 500g)

6 large spring onions

1 level tsp salt

½ level tsp caster sugar

1 level tsp finely chopped ginger, fresh or bottled

3 tblsp soy sauce

Cantonese Sea Bass with Onions and Ginger

With sea bass costing almost half as much again as fresh salmon, this is a luxury which the Chinese cherish. It is usual to serve it with other dishes as part of a complete Chinese meal and two fish should be adequate for several portions. It is ideal for the microwave, tender and delicious, and discreetly understated.

1. Have fish gutted but leave on heads. Wash and paper dry then make 3 diagonal cuts on either side of body, each about 1 inch (2½cm) apart.

2. Place head to tail in a fairly shallow dish measuring about 12 by 8 inches (30 by 20cm).

3. Trim onions, leaving 3 inches (8cm) of green on each. Cut lengthwise into hair thin threads. (A slow job but worthwhile.) Sprinkle over the fish.

4. Mix together rest of ingredients and spoon over fish. Cover with cling wrap, nick twice and cook 12 minutes, turning dish round once.

5. Transfer to an oval platter and coat fish with onions and liquid from dish.

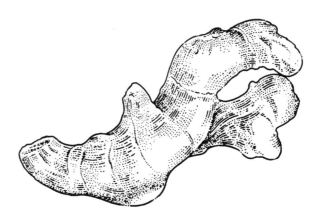

Chinese Fresh Noodles

Serves 4–6
Power Level Full
Cooking Time 8 minutes

1lb (450g) Chinese fresh noodles

1½pt (900ml) boiling water

2 level tsp salt

1 tsp sesame oil

Seek these out if you are near an Oriental shop. They are a warm yellow colour due to the addition of eggs and have a special flavour all their own.

1. Put noodles into a deep dish. Add boiling water and salt then stir well to mix.

2. Leave uncovered and cook 7 minutes. Drain thoroughly then toss with sesame oil. Reheat 1 minute, uncovered.

Chinese Dried Noodles

Available in packets from most supermarket chains, cook as directed on the packet, doing so in the microwave instead of conventionally. Keep uncovered to prevent boiling over. There is minimal time saving but a substantial reduction in fuel costs.

Serves 6
Power Level Full
Cooking Time 22 minutes

1³/4pt (1 litre) clear chicken
soup or poultry stock

1 can (about 7oz or 225g)
water chestnuts

1 can (about 7oz or 225g)
sliced bamboo shoots in water

3oz (75g) button mushrooms

½ packet (5oz or 150g) tofu
(soybean curd available in
blocks from good health food
stores)

1 can (about 6oz or 150g)
crab in brine

To thicken and flavour

1 level tblsp cornflour

1 tblsp cold water

2 tblsp vinegar

1 tblsp soy sauce

1 tsp sesame oil

½ to 1 level tsp salt

1 egg (Grade 1 or 2), beaten

Hot and Sour Crab Soup

A Chinese classic and a feature of quality
Oriental restaurants. Fortunately, it's fairly easy
to copy economically at home and this
microwave version is excellent.

1. Pour soup or stock into a *large* bowl. Drain
   water chestnuts and coarsely chop. Add, with
   liquid from can, to soup with bamboo shoots
   and their liquor.

2. Trim mushrooms, wipe clean, slice thinly and
   add to bowl. Cut bean curd into small cubes
   and coarsely mash crab in its own liquor. Add
   both to bowl. Cover with cling wrap, nick
   twice and cook 15 minutes. Uncover and stir
   round.

3. Meanwhile, mix cornflour smoothly with
   water. Stir in vinegar, soy sauce, oil, salt and
   egg. Add to soup or stock mixture, cover as
   above and continue to cook a further 7
   minutes. Stir round, cover with a plate and
   stand 2 minutes.

4. Adjust salt to taste if necessary and serve
   piping hot in warm bowls.

29

Glazed Monkfish with Green Beans

Serves 4–6
Power Level Full
Cooking Time 9½ minutes

4oz (125g) French beans
¼pt (150ml) boiling water
1lb (450g) monkfish or pieces of monkfish
1 level tblsp cornflour
¼ level tsp five spice powder
3 tblsp medium sherry or Chinese rice wine
2 tsp Chinese oyster sauce (available in bottles)
½ tsp sesame oil
1 garlic clove, peeled and crushed
2 fluid oz (50ml) hot water
1 tblsp soy sauce

Look out for monkfish pieces to make this classic Chinese fish combination economically. Serve with egg noodles.

1. Wash beans then top and tail. Cut each one in half. Put into a 2pt (1¼ litre) dish, add water, cover with cling wrap and nick twice.

2. Cook 4 minutes and drain. Leave aside for the time being. Wash monkfish or monkfish pieces and cut into strips.

3. Mix cornflour and spice powder smoothly with sherry or rice wine then stir in rest of ingredients. Transfer to dish, cook 1½ minutes then again stir until smooth.

4. Add beans and monkfish. Cover as above and cook 4 minutes. Stand 2 minutes. Stir round and serve.

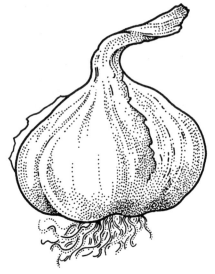

Red-Cooked Chicken

Serves 4
Power Level Full
Cooking Time 26 minutes

6 Chinese dried mushrooms
Hot water
8 chicken drumsticks (2lb or 1kg)
1 garlic clove, peeled and crushed
4oz (125g) onions, peeled and grated
1 slightly rounded tblsp finely chopped ginger, fresh or bottled
3 fluid oz (75ml) medium sherry
1 level tsp black treacle
2 level tsp finely grated tangerine peel
2 fluid oz (50ml) soy sauce

Red-cooking is basically a sophisticated form of Chinese stewing, the food becoming deep mahogany red as it simmers with soy sauce, spices, sugar and tangerine peel. Made correctly, it is complex for a Westerner to emulate convincingly but my adaptation is a reasonable copy of the real thing, fragrantly scented and pleasingly edible. One warning: the dish is salty so serve with plenty of rice.

1. Wash mushrooms then soak in hot water for 30 minutes. Drain and cut into strips.

2. Wash and dry drumsticks, slash fleshy part of each in 2 places and arrange in a 10-inch (25cm) round dish, bony ends pointing towards centre.

3. Cover with cling wrap, nick twice and cook 12 minutes, turning dish twice. Mix together rest of ingredients and spoon over chicken. Cover as above and cook a further 14 minutes. Stand 5 minutes before serving.

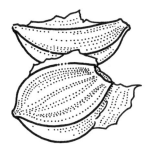

31

Serves 6
Power Level Full
Cooking Time 25–27
minutes

1oz (25g) Chinese dried mushrooms

½pt (275ml) boiling water

---

6 spring onions

---

1 tblsp peanut oil

---

12 chicken wings (2lb or 1kg), washed and dried

---

1 can (8oz or 225g) sliced bamboo shoots and their liquid

---

2 level tblsp cornflour

---

3 tblsp Chinese rice wine or medium sherry

---

4 tblsp soy sauce

---

1 level tsp salt

---

1 level tsp finely chopped ginger, fresh or bottled

Regal Chicken Wings

A refined and delicately-flavoured chicken dish which dates back to the latter half of the last century. It was much favoured by the Chinese elite and then, as now, was eaten with rice or Chinese noodles.

1. Wash mushrooms well, put into a bowl and cover with boiling water. Soak 30 minutes, drain and cut each into halves or quarters, depending on size.

2. Trim and coarsely chop onions. Put into a 10-inch (30cm) dish with oil. Leave uncovered and cook 3 minutes. Stir round then arrange chicken wings in dish, leaving a small hollow in the centre. Cover with cling wrap, nick twice and cook 12 minutes.

3. Uncover chicken and coat with bamboo shoots and liquid from can. Scatter cut up mushrooms over the top.

4. In small bowl, blend cornflour smoothly with wine or sherry. Add rest of ingredients and spoon over chicken. Cover as above and cook a further 10 to 12 minutes or until liquid is bubbling. Stand 5 minutes before serving.

Rollmop Salad with Apples (p 117)
(Photo: Sea Fish Industry Authority)

Overleaf, above: Jambalaya with Chicken (p 147)
(Photo: Tilda Rice)
Overleaf, below: Tacos (p 151)
(Photo: Old El Paso Information Services)

CHINA-ENGLAND

Serves 3
Power Level Full
Cooking Time 16 minutes

6 fleshy chicken thighs (1lb 10oz or 725g)

4oz (125g) sweetcorn, partially thawed if frozen

4oz (125g) cut leeks, partially thawed if frozen

3 generous tblsp Classic Chinese Marinade

Marinaded Chicken with Sweetcorn and Leek

A cheat's delight, tasting as authentic as anything from a quality Chinese restaurant. The trick here for speed is to use ready-prepared bought marinade and two vegetables with the chicken. The microwave will do the rest.

1. Wash and dry chicken and put into a fairly deep bowl.

2. Add rest of ingredients. Stir well to mix, cover with a plate and leave in the refrigerator for 2 to 3 hours.

3. Before cooking, stir ingredients then transfer to a 9-inch (23cm) round dish, placing chicken against edges.

4. Cover with cling wrap, nick twice and cook 16 minutes, turning 4 times. Stand 5 minutes before serving with Chinese noodles (page 28).

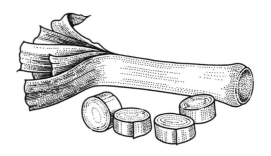

Serves 4
Power Level Full
Cooking Time 10 minutes

1lb (450 to 500g) chicken breasts

3oz (75g) red pepper

1 celery stalk

2 large spring onions

3 tblsp Chilli and garlic marinade

Marinaded Chilli Chicken

A variation of the first marinaded chicken, this one is tastefully spiced and relatively low calorie.

1. Skin chicken breasts if necessary then cut flesh into narrow strips.

2. Wash and de-seed red pepper. Scrub celery clean under cold water. Trim onions. Slice all the vegetables thinly.

3. Put vegetables into a bowl with chicken, add marinade and mix well. Cover with a plate and leave in the refrigerator for 2 to 3 hours.

4. Cook as previous recipe in an 8-inch (20cm) dish, allowing 10 minutes.

EUROPE-
CENTRAL AND
EASTERN

Serves 6
Power Level Full
Cooking Time 15 minutes

1½lb (675g) celeriac
4 tblsp cold water
1 tblsp lemon juice
I level tsp salt
Mayonnaise with flavouring

Celeriac Salad

An 'on the side dish', designed for cold meat and poultry. The lemon juice helps to prevent the celeriac from browning while it cooks.

1. Peel celeriac thickly. Slice thinly and put into a fairly large, round dish.

2. Mix together remaining ingredients except mayonaise. Pour over celeriac, cover with cling wrap and nick twice.

3. Cook 15 minutes. Drain and toss while hot with mayonnaise flavoured with mustard or garlic. Serve warm or cold. Do not chill.

Kohl-rabi Salad
Follow above recipe exactly, substituting kohl-rabi for celeriac. Cover and cook 17 minutes at full power.

Hot Celeriac with Hollandaise Sauce
Cook celeriac as for salad, drain and serve hot with Hollandaise Sauce.

Note

Celeriac

This is a variety of celery with a swede-shaped root and a thick, brown skin. It is readily available from supermarkets. It tastes like a celery-flavoured potato.

Kohl-rabi

A member of the cabbage family, the vegetable grows above ground and has a turnip-shaped root. It tastes faintly of turnip.

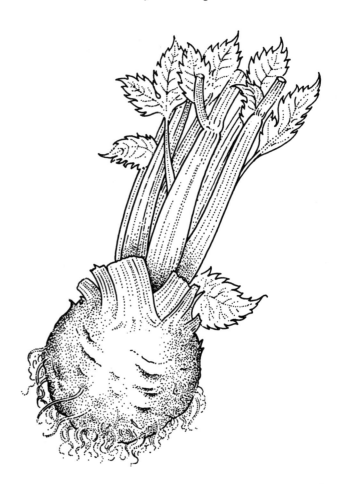

EUROPE- NORTH AND CENTRAL

Serves 3
Power Level Full
Cooking Time 28 minutes

1 carp, medium size and sliced into 6 pieces
Cold water
Vinegar
9oz (250g) onions
8oz (225g) carrots
1pt (575ml) boiling water
½ level tsp saffron strands (optional)
2 to 3 level tsp salt

Poached Carp in Jelly

The Germans celebrate with it, the Czechs queue for it, the Poles revere it, the Hungarians paprika it, the Asians wok it, the Israelis farm it to keep up supplies and occasionally I buy it in my local market or exotic fish shop for novelty. Like all river fish, carp is bony and an acquired taste though its delicacy of flavour can be likened to that of trout. My recipe is pretty standard of its type and if you'd like to have a go, seek out an obliging fishmonger who will clean and scale the carp and cut the thing up into slices. Also persuade him to remove the tail and fins.

For interest only, carp is a fresh water fish, a sort of member of the goldfish family. In common with other fresh water fish, carp should be eaten as fresh as possible.

1. Wash and dry carp. Soak in water soured with vinegar for 3 hours to minimise any

muddy after-taste and remove blood. Drain
and refrigerate until needed.

2. Peel onions and carrots then finely chop both.
   Put into a 9-inch (23cm) round dish with
   water, saffron if used and the salt. Cover with
   cling wrap, nick twice and cook 20 minutes.
   Turn dish 4 times.

3. Drain thoroughly, discarding vegetables.
   Return liquid to dish, add carp and cover as
   above. Cook 8 minutes, turning twice.

4. Stand 3 minutes then carefully remove fish to
   a shallow dish. Refrigerate, covered, when
   just cold. Pour liquid into a jug and
   refrigerate until lightly jellied (which it does
   by itself).

5. Remove layer of fat and spoon jelly over carp.

FRANCE

Cod in Cider Sauce

Serves 4
Power Level Full
Cooking Time 11 – 11½ minutes

3oz (75g) onions

6oz (175g) carrots

2oz (50g) butter or margarine

2oz (50g) button mushrooms, trimmed

---

4 cod or hake steaks, each 6 to 8oz (175 to 225g)

---

1 level tsp salt

¼pt (150ml) medium cider or apple juice

---

2 level tsp cornflour

---

1 tblsp cold water

A lively way with cod from Normandy which is distinctively poached in cider and packed with vegetables. If children are involved, substitute apple juice for cider. Serve with creamed potatoes and mange tout or fresh peas.

1. Peel onions, cut into very thin slices then separate slices into rings. Peel carrots and cut into hair thin slices.

2. Melt half the butter or margarine in an 8-inch (20cm) dish. Allow about 1 minute and leave uncovered.

3. Add onions and carrots then slice in the mushrooms. Wash and dry fish then arrange on top. Sprinkle with salt then pour in the cider or juice. Dot with rest of butter or margarine.

4. Cover with cling wrap, nick twice and cook 8

minutes, turning dish 4 times. Carefully strain off cooking liquid and leave on one side.

5. In measuring cup, mix cornflour smoothly with water. Pour in the fish liquor and cook, uncovered, for about 2 to 2½ minutes until thickened. Whisk at the end of every minute.

6. Arrange vegetables on top of fish then coat with sauce.

Serves about 8
Power Level Defrost
Cooking Time 20 minutes

6oz (175g) pigs' liver

4oz (125g) lean pork

4oz (125g) gammon

2oz (50g) onion, peeled and quartered

1 garlic clove, peeled

2oz (50g) fresh white breadcrumbs

¼pt (150ml) single cream

2 eggs (Grade 3)

½ level tsp salt

⅛ level tsp ground allspice

Freshly ground black pepper

French-style Country Pâté

A typical rustic pâté for which the French are so renowned. The combination of liver, fresh pork and bacon makes for a beautifully moist texture and the hint of spice is appetising without being overwhelming.

1. Brush a 7-inch (18cm) microwave plastic ring mould with oil or melted fat then line completely with cling wrap, making a small hole in the centre so that it slips over the stem of the mould.

2. Mince together first 5 ingredients. Transfer to a basin and stir in crumbs.

3. Beat cream with rest of ingredients and thoroughly mix into minced meats.

4. Spread evenly into mould, cover with cling

wrap and nick twice. Cook for 10 minutes then stand inside oven for 5 minutes. Cook a further 5 minutes. Stand for 10 minutes, cook for 5 minutes.

5. Cool in the mould then turn out when cold and refrigerate until ready to serve.

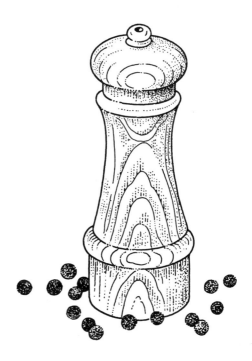

Mushrooms à la Grècque

Serves 4
Power Level Full
Cooking Time 7½ minutes

---

1 bouquet garni bag

---

1 garlic clove, peeled and crushed

---

2 bay leaves

---

4 tblsp water

---

2 tblsp fresh lemon juice, strained

---

1 tblsp vinegar

---

1 tblsp olive oil

---

1 level tsp salt

1lb (450 to 500g) very small button mushrooms, trimmed

---

2 level tblsp chopped parsley

A firmly established starter which can be found worldwide. Certainly it is much favoured in Britain and appears on many restaurant menus, especially Bistro type.

1. Put bouquet garni, garlic, bay leaves, water, lemon juice, vinegar, oil and salt into a fairly large bowl.

2. Cover with an inverted plate and heat for 4 minutes. Stir in mushrooms, again cover and cook 3½ minutes.

3. Lift mushrooms out of dish with a draining spoon and divide equally between 4 small bowls.

4. Strain the cooking liquor over mushrooms and refrigerate until well-chilled.

Mustard Tomatoes

Serves 4
Power Level Full
Cooking Time 6 minutes

---

4 large tomatoes, at kitchen temperature

Salt and pepper

---

5 generous tsp whole grain mustard

Easy elegance and a good companion to roast poultry and grilled steaks or lamb chops.

1. Wash and dry tomatoes and cut in half horizontally. Arrange round the edge of a dinner plate.

2. Sprinkle with salt and pepper then spread each half with mustard.

3. Leave uncovered and cook 6 minutes.

Serves 2
Power Level Full
Cooking Time 8 minutes

---

2 large trout, each 1lb or 450 to 500g

3oz (75g) onion, peeled

---

1 small lemon, washed and dried

---

4 small bay leaves

½ level tsp herbes de Provence

---

1 level tsp salt

Truites en Papillote

Parcels of trout, cooked to a delicate tenderness with fresh lemon, onion and herbs. The only addition for perfection is a 'sauce' of melted butter (or sunflower margarine if preferred). A tablespoon of chopped parsley or fresh tarragon may be added. New potatoes and broccoli are ideal accompaniments.

1. Have ready 2 pieces of parchment paper, each about 16 by 14 inches (42 by 36cm).

2. Clean trout (or get fishmonger to do this for you) but leave on heads to prevent trout from shrinking.

3. Slice onion and lemon to medium thickness. Pack into slit cavities of fish, adding 2 bay leaves to each. Place on paper.

4. Sprinkle with herbs and salt. Wrap individually but put both parcels on to one plate. Cook 8 minutes.

5. Stand 2 minutes then open out on to 2 warm plates, removing paper.

FRANCE-BELGIUM

Serves 4
Power Level Full
Cooking Time 12 minutes

Moules Marinières

Devotees of mussels will always be tempted by this shellfish classic, never better than when given the microwave treatment.

2pt (900ml) (approximately 1¹/₂lb (675g)) fresh mussels

¹/₂oz (15g) butter or margarine

1 small onion, peeled and finely chopped

1 garlic clove, peeled and crushed

¹/₄pt (150ml) dry white wine

1 bouquet garni sachet

1 bay leaf

1 to 1¹/₂ level tsp salt

4 level tblsp fresh white breadcrumbs

3 level tblsp finely chopped parsley

1. Wash mussels under cold running water. Scrape away any barnacles and trim away the 'beards'. Discard any mussels with cracked or opened shells as these are dangerous. Give mussels a second wash.

2. Put butter or margarine into a deep dish. Melt for 1 minute. Stir in onion and garlic. Cover with an inverted plate and cook for 6 minutes, stirring twice.

3. Add wine, bouquet garni sachet, bay leaf, salt and mussels. Cover as before and cook 5 minutes.

4. Scoop mussels into 4 bowls and stir breadcrumbs and half the parsley into liquor. Pour over mussels and sprinkle rest of parsley over each serving.

FRANCE - NOUVELLE CUISINE

Serves 6–8
Power Level Full
Cooking Time 4 minutes

12oz (350g) fresh raspberries

3 level tblsp icing sugar

1 level tblsp cornflour

5 tblsp hot water

Raspberry Coulis

The 'underneath' sauce, used by top chefs to line a plate and decorate the top with artistic arrangements of fruit, cream, little pastry cases, meringues, custards and other personal creations. For home use, it can be floated on to plates and topped with strawberries and cream, peach and kiwi slices, strips of pineapple with sorbet, assorted berry fruits and shortbread biscuits. It looks classy.

1. Rub raspberries through a fine mesh sieve directly into a bowl.

2. Sift in icing sugar and cornflour. Gently beat in water. Cook 4 minutes, whisking at the end of every minute.

3. Strain again, cover and leave until cold before using.

Soft Berry Coulis
Any other soft berry fruits may be used instead of the raspberries.

FRANCE - INTERNATIONAL

Serves 6
Power Level Full
Cooking Time 21–24 minutes

Shortcrust pastry made from 6oz (175g) plain flour

3oz (75g) mixture of margarine and cooking fat

1 egg yolk

Custard Filling

8oz (225g) lean bacon rashers without rind

3 eggs (Grade 3)

½pt (275ml) rich milk or single cream

½ level tsp salt

Nutmeg

Quiche Lorraine

Quiche is everywhere and though different from the original tart cooked in Lorraine with bacon and an egg custard on top, it is always greatly appreciated whichever way it comes. I start off with the original and follow with a selection of variations.

1. Roll out pastry fairly thinly on a floured surface. Use to line an 8-inch (20cm) china or glass flan dish.

2. Prick well all over, particularly where base and sides of pastry meet. Leave uncovered and cook 6 minutes, turning dish 4 times. Brush with egg yolk and cook 1 minute, uncovered.

3. Arrange bacon rashers on a plate lined with paper towels. Cover with more towels and cook 4 to 5 minutes or until obviously ready.

4. Drain and cool slightly. Cut each rasher in half and arrange over base of pastry case.

5. Beat eggs well with milk or cream, season with salt and pour over bacon.

6. Sprinkle with nutmeg and cook 10 to 12 minutes or until bubbles just begin to break across the centre. Turn 4 times and leave to stand at least 10 minutes before cutting. Serve warm or cold.

Prawn Quiche

Cover base of Quiche with 6oz (175g) peeled prawns instead of bacon. Add ½ level tsp finely grated lemon peel to the custard mixture.

Tomato Quiche

Cover base of Quiche with 6oz (175g) skinned and sliced tomatoes instead of bacon. Sprinkle ½ level tsp dried basil over the top.

Niçoise Quiche

Cover base of Quiche with 1 small can drained and flaked tuna, 1½oz (40g) pitted black olives and 1 level tblsp tomato purée dotted over the top.

Spinach Quiche

Cover base of Quiche with 6oz (175g) cooked spinach from which the water has literally been wrung out. It must be as dry as possible.

Serves 4
Power Level Defrost
Cooking Time 3 minutes

12 small leaves near heart of Dutch lettuce

1 box mustard and cress

1 bunch, bundle or bag of watercress (it is usually sold in bags in supermarkets)

1 whole soft goat cheese as decribed above

Dressing

6 tblsp grapeseed oil

6 tsp hazelnut oil

2 tsp orange flower water

2 level tsp Dijon mustard

3 tblsp raspberry vinegar

Warm Salad of Leaves with Goat Cheese

Gastronomic licence with this modern classic in that I have chosen a splendid pepper covered and garlic-flavoured goat cheese from Gloucester – round, robust, fairly thick and about 4 inches (10cm) in diameter – which is made in Tewkesbury by Bredons Norton Dairy Farm in Bredons Norton. The dressing is all mine and its forceful character matches the cheese.

1. Wash and dry lettuce leaves. Leave mustard and cress in its box, wash well, shake dry and cut off stems level to the top of box. Wash and drain watercress.

2. Arrange lettuce leaves and the two cresses attractively on 4 fairly large plates – the artistic interpretation is up to individual taste.

3. Slice cheese in half horizontally then cut each half into 6 wedges. Place 4 wedges on to each plate.

4. Pour remaining ingredients into a jug. Leave uncovered and heat for 3 minutes. Stir round and trickle over salads. Eat straight away.

GERMANY

4 eggs (Grade 2)
5oz (150g) caster sugar
1 tsp vanilla essence
2 level tsp cornflour
¼pt (150ml) sweet white wine
¼pt (150ml) double cream
2 tblsp brandy

Berlin Air

Fluffy, light and whimsical, characteristic of pre World War Two life in Berlin when everything was sweet.

1. Whisk eggs and sugar together in a large bowl until they bulk up to about 2 to 2½ pints (1.2 to 1.25 litres). Beat in vanilla.

2. Mix cornflour smoothly with a little wine. Stir in rest of wine then add to egg mixture.

3. Leave uncovered and cook 3½ minutes, whisking at the end of every ½ minute. When ready, mixture should be thick and foamy and cling to the whisk like custard. Cover and leave until completely cold.

4. Beat cream and brandy well together until thick. Gently whisk into egg mixture.

5. Transfer to 6 small dishes and refrigerate until well chilled. Serve with wafer biscuits or soft berry fruits.

GREAT BRITAIN

1 large cauliflower weighing
1¼lb or 575g after trimming

1 level tsp salt

¼pt (150ml) hot water

1oz (25g) plain flour

1 level tsp powder mustard

¼pt (150ml) milk or single
cream

4oz (125g) grated Cheddar
cheese

4 tblsp hot water

Cauliflower Cheese

Always a favourite for lunch or as an
accompaniment to roast meat and poultry,
Cauliflower Cheese is a very British institution,
nostalgic in its own way and handsomely
flavoured. It is popular with vegetarians and
should be served with brown bread toast.

1. Wash cauliflower and put into a fairly roomy
   bowl, head uppermost. Mix salt and water
   together then pour over.

2. Cover with cling wrap, nick twice and cook
   10 minutes at full.

3. Meanwhile, tip flour and mustard into a small
   bowl and *very gradually* work in cold milk or
   single cream. If any lumps form, break down
   with the back of a spoon.

4. Take cauliflower out of oven, keep hot and
   carefully drain cooking liquor into the flour
   mixture. Whisk until smooth, leave
   uncovered and cook 4 to 5 minutes at full
   power, whisking three times.

5. Stir in cheese and hot water. Cook 1½ minutes at defrost. Spoon over cauliflower and serve straight away.

Serves 1
Power Level Full
Cooking Time 5 minutes

1 large kipper (450 to 500g or 1lb)

4 fluid oz (120ml) cold water

The Kipper

Kippers are a very British thing, often served for breakfast in the old days when the life style was more leisured. Some hotel and bed and breakfast places still do offer you a kipper as a substitute for the traditional bacon and egg fry-up but it often turns up frizzled and salty after an unkind grilling. The microwave approach is altogether gentler and the fishy smell is well-contained within the confines of the oven. Try it and see.

1. Cut off kipper tail and soak fish in plenty of cold water for a minimum of 3 to 4 hours as this sometimes helps to reduce saltiness.

2. Place diagonally across the base of an 8-inch (20cm) square dish, fairly shallow, then add the water.

3. Cover with cling wrap, nick twice and cook 4 minutes. Drain, slide kipper on to a plate and serve straight away, topped with a knob of butter or margarine.

Tip
Lemon juice, squeezed over the kipper, enlivens the taste.

51

Potted Kipper

1. Cook 1 large kipper, of about 1lb or 450 to 500g, as directed in The Kipper recipe (page 51).

2. Remove skin and take flesh off bones. Put into blender or food processor with 3oz (75g) softened butter or margarine, 1 tblsp lemon juice, freshly milled black pepper, 1 level tsp prepared English mustard and a shake or two of Worcester sauce.

3. Work to a smooth paste, spoon into a dish and cover. Refrigerate until firm. Use as a spread for hot toast.

Serves 4
Power Level Full
Cooking Time 18–20½ minutes

Gooseberry Sauce
12oz (350g) gooseberries
4 tblsp boiling water
1 slightly rounded tblsp caster sugar
½ level tsp finely grated lemon peel

Mackerel
4 Mackerel, each 8oz or 225g, gutted and cleaned
2oz (50g) butter or margarine

Mackerel with Gooseberry Sauce

A taste of Old England, well worth reviving in late spring, early summer, when gooseberries make their annual appearance. The sauce has a refreshing piquancy that goes particularly well with the mackerel.

1. Top and tail gooseberries, wash well and put into a dish with water. Cover with cling wrap and nick twice.

2. Cook 6 minutes, turning dish 3 times. Uncover, mash down well then stir in sugar and lemon peel. Cover as before and cook a further 1½ minutes. Leave aside temporarily.

3. Wash mackerel and arrange, head to tail, in a

1 tblsp lemon juice

Salt and pepper to taste

greased dish measuring about 8 by 10 inches (20 by 25cm).

4. Put butter or margarine in a dish and melt 1½ to 2 minutes. Stir in lemon juice and pour over fish. Sprinkle with salt and pepper to taste.

5. Cover with cling wrap, nick twice and cook for 8 to 10 minutes or until skin begins to break. Leave to stand for 5 minutes.

6. Reheat sauce for 1 minute. Transfer mackerel to 4 warm plates and pass the gooseberry sauce separately in a bowl.

**Serves allow 6oz (175g) raw weight per person minimum
Power Level Full
Cooking Time 9 minutes per lb (450g)**

Roast Leg of Pork with Crackling

Pork does crackle in the microwave due to the long length of cooking time – more than chicken – at 9 minutes to the pound (or 450g). The fat should be deeply scored and sprinkled thickly with salt before cooking.

Choose a piece of leg, size to suit, then wash and dry. Place in a dish or on a trivet in a dish. Sprinkle with salt then 'open' roast by covering joint with a piece of non-stick parchment paper. Turn dish 4 times while cooking and, like chicken, 'rest' joint halfway through.

At the very end, lift pork on to a carving board, cover with foil and leave to stand for 8 minutes. Accompany with sage and onion stuffing balls and roast potatoes.

Boned and Rolled Joints without Bone

Cook as pork but do not sprinkle with salt. Allow 9 minutes per pound (450g) for veal, ham and lamb and 6 to 8 minutes for beef, depending on how well done you like it to be. Put into dish, cover with cling wrap and nick twice. Cook for required number of minutes, turning dish 4 to 5 times and allowing joint to rest halfway through like the chicken. At the very end, lift joint on to a carving board, cover with foil and leave to stand from 5 to 8 minutes, depending on size.

Serves 4
Power Level Full
Cooking Time 6½ minutes

6oz (175g) self raising flour

½ level tsp salt

2oz (50g) shredded suet

---

6 tblsp cold water

1¼lb (675g) home stewed steak and kidney (or canned), heated until hot

---

Steak and Kidney Pudding

As British as John Bull, this unique pudding is an international talking point and has a happy relationship with the microwave.

As meat cooked in water toughens in the microwave, I suggest you stew the steak and kidney in the conventional way or use canned varieties. Either way it should be hot before going into pie.

1. Well grease a 1½pt (900ml) pudding basin.

2. Sift flour and salt into a bowl. Toss in suet

then add cold water, stirring with a fork to make a fairly soft and pliable dough.

3. Roll out into a 12-inch (30cm) round. Using a sharp knife, cut out a ¼ of the circle and reserve for lid.

4. Line basin with remaining pastry, pressing out wrinkles and easing it over base and sides until it reaches the inner rim. Seal pastry joins together with dampened fingers.

5. Fill with hot meat filling, wet edges of lining pastry with a brush dipped in water then cover with a lid rolled from reserved pastry. Pinch pastry edges together to seal.

6. Cover with cling wrap, nick twice and cook 6½ minutes when pastry should be well-risen. Stand 5 minutes, uncover and spoon out on to plates.

Cherries in Port Wine Jelly

Serves 6
Power Level Defrost and Full
Cooking Time 3½–4 minutes

1 jar (1½lb or 675 to 680g) pitted morello cherries (or the same weight in cans or jars of any other cherries, provided they are pitted)

1 envelope gelatine

3 tblsp caster sugar

Port

A winter sweet with an air of exclusivity, a beauty for any festive season but Christmas especially when the port's to hand and the mood is merry. It's also easy to make.

1. Strain cherries, reserving syrup. Pour 2 tblsp into 2½pt (1¼ litre) basin and stir in the gelatine. Soften for 2 minutes. Cover with an inverted saucer and melt for 2 minutes at defrost.

2. Stir round to make sure gelatine has melted. If

55

not, return to microwave and heat for an extra ½ minute, checking every 10 seconds.

3. Mix in rest of cherry syrup and sugar. Make up to ¾pt (450ml) with port. Cover as above and heat 1½ minutes at full power. Again stir round to make sure sugar has melted.

4. Cool to room temperature then refrigerate until just beginning to thicken and set. Fold in cherries, transfer to a water-rinsed jelly mould and refrigerate until firm. Unmould on to a plate.

5. Accompany with whipped cream dusted with cinnamon or nutmeg.

To make life easy
Set jelly in 6 small dishes and mound each with whipped cream before serving.

An alternative
Instead of cream, serve jelly with cold stewed apples which have been blended to a purée and flavoured with grated orange peel.

Christmas Pudding

Serves 12 – makes 2 puddings
Power Level Full
Cooking Time 6 minutes per pudding

2½oz (65g) plain flour

---

1 level tblsp cocoa powder

The microwave weaves its own spell of magic in the way it cooks Christmas puddings. It takes minutes instead of hours in the steamer and the end result tastes as luscious as it looks.

1. Brush 2 basins, each 1½pt or ¾ litre, with melted fat.

1 level tsp allspice or mixed spice
1 level tsp finely grated orange or tangerine peel
3oz (85g) fresh brown breadcrumbs
4oz (125g) dark brown soft sugar
6oz (175g) currants
3oz (75 to 80g) sultanas
3oz (75 to 80g) seedless raisins
2oz (50g) chopped prunes or dates
2oz (50g) mixed chopped peel
4oz (125g) suet (vegetarian for health if preferred)
2 eggs (Grade 3), at kitchen temperature and beaten
3 tsp black treacle
4 tblsp stout or something like Norfolk Punch
1 tblsp milk

2. Sift first 3 ingredients into a bowl. Add peel, crumbs, sugar, dried fruits, peel, suet, eggs, treacle, stout and milk.

3. Fork mix to a soft consistency and divide equally between prepared basins. Cover with cling wrap and nick twice.

4. Cook 4 minutes, turning twice. Rest 4 minutes in the microwave then continue to cook for another 2 minutes. Turn out and serve. Alternatively, cool completely, wrap in parchment paper and overwrap in foil. Freeze until needed. Defrost before serving, cut into portions and cook each one for a few seconds or until you can see the fruit just beginning to bubble. Serve with Brandy Sauce (page 58).

Brandy Sauce

Serves 6
Power Level Full
Cooking Time 6–7 minutes

1 oz (25g) butter or margarine

1oz (25g) plain flour

½pt (275ml) lukewarm milk

2 level tblsp caster sugar

1 to 2 level tblsp brandy

1. Put butter or margarine into a bowl, leave uncovered and melt 1 minute. Stir in flour then gradually whisk in milk.

2. Return to microwave and cook 5 to 6 minutes when sauce should come to the boil and thicken. Whisk well at the end of every minute to prevent lumps from forming.

3. Stir in sugar and brandy, transfer to a jug and serve with the pudding.

Plum Crumble

Serves 4–6
Power Level Full
Cooking Time 15 minutes

1lb (450 to 500g) plums, weight AFTER stoning

4oz (125g) soft brown sugar

Topping

6oz (175g) brown plain flour

4oz (125g) butter or margarine

3oz (75g) soft brown sugar

An old time favourite, in its glory with custard or cream.

1. Place fruit and sugar in a 1¾pt (1 litre) greased shallow dish and toss over and over to combine.

2. For crumble topping, tip flour into a bowl. Rub in butter or margarine finely. Fork in sugar then sprinkle mixture evenly over fruit.

3. Cook 15 minutes, turning dish 3 times. Stand 3 minutes before serving.

GREAT BRITAIN-SCOTLAND

Serves 8
Power Level Full
Cooking Time 33 minutes

1½lb (675 to 700g) chicken
joints

---

4 medium leeks (1½lb or 675
to 700g)

2pt (1.2 litres) hot water

---

2 level tsp salt

---

1 bouquet garni sachet

2oz (50g) long grain rice

---

12 stoned and halved prunes

Cock-a-Leekie Soup

Probably as old as the Scottish hills themselves,
this warming chicken and leek soup has a fine,
rich flavour and the addition of prunes gives it a
unique and unusual touch.

1. Wash and dry chicken and place in an 8-inch
   (20cm) dish. Cover with cling wrap, nick
   twice and cook 12 minutes.

2. Meanwhile, prepare leeks. Slit and
   thoroughly wash then coarsely shred.

3. Remove chicken from dish, reserving liquor.
   Take meat off bones

4. Pour water into a deep dish. Add salt,
   bouquet garni sachet, rice, leeks and reserved
   chicken liquor. Cover with an inverted plate
   and cook 18 minutes.

5. Stir in chicken pieces and prunes. Cover again
   and reheat 3 minutes.

Scotch Broth

Serves 6
Power Level Full
Cooking Time 29–34 minutes

½oz (15g) pearl barley

Cold water

8oz (225g) neck of lamb fillet

2pt (1.2 litres) boiling water

4oz (125g) onions, peeled and chopped

2oz (50g) carrot, peeled and cut into small cubes

2oz (50g) turnip, peeled and cut into small cubes

---

1 small leek, slit, well-washed then cut into fine shreds

---

1 to 1½ level tsp salt

Freshly ground black pepper

Heartwarming and inviting, this is one of the top soups from Scotland, a joy in the winter and sustaining with fresh brown bread.

1. Tip barley into a bowl, add 4 tblsp cold water, cover with an inverted plate and leave to soften for 4 hours in the kitchen.

2. Prior to making soup, cut fat off lamb and discard. Cut meat into very small cubes – rather like coarse mince.

3. Put into a 4pt (2.25 litre) bowl with boiling water and drained barley. Cover with an inverted plate and cook 4 minutes. Skim off scum.

4. Add all remaining vegetables, cover with cling wrap, nick twice and cook for 25 to 30 minutes or until barley, meat and vegetables are soft.

5. Stand 5 minutes, stir round and serve. If liked, sprinkle each serving with chopped parsley.

GREAT BRITAIN- WALES

Shearing Cake

Serves 8
Power Level Full
Cooking Time 5 minutes

8oz (225g) self raising flour

4oz (125g) butter or margarine

6oz (175g) light brown soft sugar

Finely grated peel of 1 medium lemon

1 level tblsp caraway seeds

½ level tsp grated nutmeg

2 beaten eggs (Grade 3)

¼pt (150ml) cold milk

Lemon icing

2oz (50g) icing sugar

2 tsp lemon juice

I wonder how many of you remember speckly seed cake from childhood with its slight spiciness and tang of lemon? A reminder from Wales may evoke sweet thoughts and happy teatime memories. Try it.

1. Line an 8-inch (20cm) round dish with cling wrap, the depth of which should be about 3 inches (8cm).

2. Sift flour into a bowl. Rub in butter or margarine finely then toss in sugar, lemon peel, caraway seeds and nutmeg.

3. Beat eggs and milk well together. Fork-stir into dry ingredients to make a fairly soft mixture.

4. Transfer to prepared dish, cover with cling wrap and nick twice. Cook 5 minutes, turning dish 3 times. Stand 10 minutes then

turn out on a wire rack and leave until completely cold.

5. Carefully turn right way up. For icing, sift sugar into a bowl. Work in lemon juice and stir until smooth. Drizzle over cake and leave to set before cutting.

GREAT BRITAIN- INTERNATIONAL

Serves 4
Power Level Full
Cooking Time 10 minutes

Salmon

4 salmon steaks, each 6 to 7oz (175 to 200g)

¼pt (150ml) water or dry white wine

½ level tsp salt

Hollandaise Sauce

4 oz (125g) unsalted butter

1 tblsp fresh lemon juice, strained

2 egg yolks (Grade 3), at kitchen temperature

A pinch of caster sugar

White pepper and salt to taste

Poached Salmon with Hollandaise Sauce

There is nothing to equal Scottish salmon for quality and taste and the microwave treats the fish with the love and understanding it deserves. This beauty is an old time classic, served with pomp and circumstance in many a good restaurant and quite easy to emulate in the home kitchen by any capable cook.

Hollandaise Sauce
A glory of egg yellow, thick and glowing, gently warm and the perfect partner for salmon. Usually a painstaking job cooked conventionally but child's play in the microwave. And fast.

1. To cook fish, arrange steaks round the sides of an 8-inch (20cm) dish. Add water or wine and sprinkle salmon with salt.

2. Cover with cling wrap, nick twice and cook for 8 minutes or until just cooked. Leave to stand for 5 to 6 minutes.

3. To make sauce, cut butter into a measuring jug or small bowl, leave uncovered and heat 1½ minutes or until it looks foamy.

4. Add lemon juice and egg yolks. Whisk in well. Cook 30 to 35 seconds, remove from oven and whisk until smooth – the consistency should be like medium-thick custard. If too thin, return to oven and heat between 5 to 10 seconds; if too thick, beat in a little boiling water.

5. To serve, lift salmon out of dish with a perforated slice, transfer to 4 warm plates and coat with warm sauce.

Above: Tostados (p 152)
(Photo: Old El Paso Information Services)
Below: Prawns Madras (p 81)
(Photo: Sea Fish Industry Authority)

GREECE

Serves 4
Power Level Full
Cooking Time 19 minutes

2lb (1kg) chicken pieces

1/2 level tsp onion powder

2 level tblsp cornflour

3 level tblsp lemon juice,
strained if fresh

Hot water

2 egg yolks (Grade 1 or 2)

1 to 1 1/2 level tsp salt

Pasta Crema (p 95)
(Photo: Pasta Information
Centre)

Avgolemono Chicken

Avgolemono is an egg and lemon sauce particular to Greek cuisine with a fresh, slightly sharp tang and a primrose yellow colour. I suppose one could call it the country's national sauce and it also appears as Avgolemono soup with a touch of boiled rice for texture. It works especially well for chicken and you can serve it with boiled potatoes – new ones for preference – and a large mixed Greek style vegetable salad topped with squares of Feta cheese, black olives and a trickle or two of olive oil.

1. Wash and dry chicken and arrange round edges of a 10-inch (25cm) round dish. Sprinkle with onion powder. Cover with cling wrap, nick twice and cook 16 minutes. Stand 3 minutes.

2. In 1pt (575ml) measuring jug, mix cornflour smoothly with lemon juice. Strain in chicken

65

stock (there will be some in the dish after cooking the chicken) and make up to just over ½pt (275ml) with hot water.

3. Cook 3 minutes, whisking at the end of every minute. Sauce by now should have come to the boil and thickened. Beat in egg yolks, season with salt and spoon over chicken. Serve straight away.

Tip
If sauce is too thick for personal taste, thin down with an extra tblsp or two of hot water.

Serves 6 to 8
Power Level Full
Cooking Time 37½ minutes

1½ lb (675g) aubergines, topped and tailed

5 tblsp hot water

1 level tsp salt

1 tblsp fresh lemon juice

Meat layer

2oz (50g) butter or margarine

8oz (225g) onions, peeled and finely chopped

12oz (350g) cold roast beef or lamb, minced

4oz (125g) freshly made white or brown breadcrumbs

Seasoning to taste

12oz (350g) tomatoes

Moussaka

Everyone into Greek food will be familiar with this layered aubergine and minced meat dish with its topping of tomatoes and rich cheese sauce. A fast version follows as this traditional one takes a fair time to prepare and needs patience.

1. Wash and dry aubergines then thinly slice. Transfer to a large dish or bowl with water, salt and lemon juice. Cover with cling wrap, nick twice and cook 12 minutes. Remove from oven and leave to stand for 20 minutes. Drain.

2. For meat layer, put butter or margarine into a 4pt (2.25 litre) deep dish. Melt 1 minute, stir in onions, leave uncovered and cook 2 minutes. Remove from oven then fork in beef and crumbs. Season to taste.

3. Fill dish with alternate layers of aubergines and meat mixture. Blanch tomatoes, remove

Topping
³⁄₄pt (425ml) milk
1¹⁄₂oz (40g) butter or margarine
1¹⁄₂oz (40g) plain flour
3oz (75g) Cheddar cheese, grated
1 egg yolk

skins, slice to medium thickness and arrange on top.

4. For sauce, warm milk in a measuring jug for 3 minutes. Put butter or margarine into a bowl and melt, uncovered, for about 1½ minutes. Stir in flour, cook a further minute, remove from oven and gradually blend in milk. Cook 4 minutes until thick and bubbly, whisking at the end of every minute.

5. Stir in cheese and egg yolk and pour over Moussaka. Cover with cling wrap, nick twice and cook 13 minutes, turning dish 4 times. Stand 7 to 8 minutes before serving.

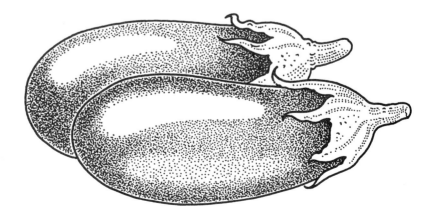

Fast Moussaka

Serves 3 to 4
Power Level Full
Cooking Time 19 minutes

---

1 aubergine weighing 8oz (225g), topped and tailed

---

1 tblsp water

½pt (275ml) cold milk

½pt (275ml) cold water

---

1 packet dried mashed potato, plain or with chopped onion

8oz (225g) cold cooked lamb or beef, minced

---

1 level tsp dried marjoram

---

1 to 1½ level tsp salt

---

2 garlic cloves, peeled and crushed

8oz (225g) tomatoes, blanched and skinned

---

4 rounded tblsp Greek yogurt

---

1 egg (Grade 3)

2oz (50g) grated Cheddar cheese

A variation on the traditional, quickly made with a packet of dried mashed potatoes, plain or with onion.

1. Wash and dry aubergine. Cut in half lengthwise and place in a shallow dish. Sprinkle with the tblsp water. Cover with cling wrap, nick twice and cook 5½ minutes. Stand 2 minutes then drain.

2. Pour milk and water into a bowl. Stir in the dried potato, cover with an inverted plate and cook for 6 minutes. Stir well then mix in lamb or beef, marjoram, salt and garlic.

3. Slice aubergine, keeping on skin. Fill a 4pt (2.25 litre) greased casserole dish with alternate layers of aubergines and potato mixture, making a centre 'sandwich filling' with half the tomatoes. End the layering with potatoes.

4. Cover with remaining tomatoes. Beat together yogurt and egg. Season to taste and pour over Moussaka. Sprinkle with cheese, cover with cling wrap as before and cook 7½ minutes. If liked, uncover and brown under the grill.

Honey Nut Cake

Serves 8–10
Power Level Medium, Full and Defrost
Cooking Time 26½ minutes

4oz (125g) unsalted English butter, at room temperature and soft

6oz (175g) light brown soft sugar

4 eggs (Grade 4), at kitchen temperature

1 tsp vanilla essence

½ level tsp soda bicarbonate

1 level tsp ground cinnamon

3oz (75g) plain flour

3oz (75g) maize flour

4oz (125g) blanched almonds, finely chopped

Syrup

½pt (275ml) water

3oz (75g) caster sugar

1 cinnamon stick

1 tsp lemon juice

5oz (150g) clear honey

1 thick slice unpeeled orange

Decoration

2oz (50g) finely chopped mixed nuts (walnuts, hazels, brazils)

2 tblsp clear honey

Sweet as sweet, drenched in syrup and studded with nuts, accept this Grecian love affair as a prize-winning dessert. Its true name is Karithopitta.

1. Have ready a 7-inch (18cm) round deep dish, well-greased and base-lined with parchment paper.

2. Put butter and sugar into a bowl and whip until light and creamy. Gradually beat in eggs and essence.

3. Using a metal spoon, fold in dry ingredients, first sifted together, then stir in the chopped almonds.

4. Transfer mixture to prepared dish, smooth top and cover with an upturned plate.

5. Cook 15 minutes at medium setting, turning twice. Cool slightly before inverting into a fairly deep dish.

6. For syrup, place all ingredients into a bowl. Cover with an upturned plate and cook 10 minutes at full power. Cool slightly, remove cinnamon stick and orange slice then spoon syrup over cake.

7. Leave until all the syrup has been absorbed. Put mixed nuts and honey into a bowl. Leave uncovered and warm through 1½ minutes at defrost. Use to decorate cake.

GREECE-
MIDDLE EAST

Dolmathes

Serves 4–6
Power Level Full
Cooking Time 31 minutes

3oz (75g) onions

1 garlic clove

1 tblsp olive oil

12oz (350g) lean minced beef

1oz (25g) long grain rice

1oz (25g) raisins

4 tblsp water

2 level tblsp chopped parsley

½ level tsp mixed spice

½ level tsp salt

Freshly ground pepper

16 vine leaves (about ½ of an 8oz or 225g packet)

Strained juice of 1 lemon

½pt (275ml) boiling water

The famous stuffed vine leaves from Greece and the Middle East cook happily in the microwave and are ready in about 30 minutes. They make an appetising hors d'oeuvre with pieces of cut-up Feta cheese, spicy olives and warm bread encrusted with sesame seeds.

1. Peel onions and finely chop or grate. Peel garlic and crush. Pour oil into a 7-inch (18cm) round dish. Add onions and garlic, cover with an inverted plate and cook for 4 minutes.

2. Stir in beef, rice, raisins, water, parsley, spice, salt and pepper. Cover as above and cook 15 minutes, stirring 4 times. Cool to lukewarm.

3. Meanwhile, soak vine leaves as directed on the packet. Drain then place smooth sides downwards on work surface. Put equal amount of meat filling on to each then roll up securely, tucking in the edges.

70

4. Pack tightly into a 10 by 6-inch (25 by 15cm) greased dish. Coat with lemon juice and water. Cover with cling wrap, nick twice and cook 12 minutes, turning dish 3 times. Leave until cold before eating.

HONG KONG

Serves 2–3
Power Level Full
Cooking Time 8 minutes

4 Chinese dried mushrooms

boiling water

4oz (125g) onions

2oz (50g) carrots

1 tblsp peanut oil

2 garlic cloves

8oz (225g) cooked chicken without bone, cut into strips

10oz (275g) bean sprouts, rinsed

1 tblsp soy sauce

1/4 tsp sesame oil

1/8 tsp cayenne pepper

1/2 to 1 level tsp salt

Chicken with Vegetables and Bean Sprouts

An appropriate choice for those who favour spicy food. It can be treated as a main course in its own right or presented with other dishes as part of an Oriental meal.

1. Put mushrooms into a bowl, cover with cold water and leave to soak for 30 minutes. Drain and cut into strips.

2. Peel and chop onions. Peel and grate carrots. Pour oil into a 3pt (1.75 litre) bowl. Add vegetables and cook, uncovered, for 3 minutes. Stir round.

3. Peel and crush garlic into bowl. Add chicken and rest of ingredients, cover with cling wrap and nick twice. Cook 5 minutes, turning bowl 3 times.

4. Stand 3 minutes, uncover, mix round and serve.

HUNGARY

Serves 4
Power Level Full
Cooking Time 1–1½
minutes (twice)

*4 large spring onions, cut to 4
inches (10cm) in length*

3oz (75g) Hungarian salami

*6oz (175g) Emmental or
Cheddar cheese, finely grated*

2 egg yolks

4 slices freshly made toast

Open Sandwiches with Cheese and Salami

I discovered these in a takeaway recipe leaflet on the counter of a Hungarian stand during a food exhibition in London. The sandwiches have a certain chic and are an up-market version of cheese on toast. The smokey taste is interesting.

1. Trim spring onions and finely chop. Remove rind from salami and chop. Put both into bowl.

2. Well mix in cheese and egg yolks. Spread thickly over the toast.

3. Leave uncovered and cook 2 at a time for 1 to 1½ minutes or until cheese melts. Serve straight away.

Paprika Potatoes

Serves 4
Power Level Full
Cooking Time 22–23 minutes

1½lb (750g) potatoes
4oz (125g) onions
2oz (50g) butter, margarine or lard
2 rounded tblsp dried mixed pepper flakes (red and green)
2 level tsp paprika
1 level tsp salt
½pt (275ml) boiling water
soured cream

Simple but fulfilling, this is an unusual potato casserole which can be treated as a vegetarian main course or side dish to go with roasts of poultry and meat. Like other members of the paprika dish family, each portion is generously topped with soured cream.

1. Peel potatoes, wash well and cut into medium-sized chunks. Peel onions and chop.

2. Put fat into a 3pt (1.75 litre) dish, leave uncovered and heat 2 to 3 minutes or until sizzling. Drain potatoes and dry. Add to dish with onions and pepper flakes.

3. Add paprika and salt to water. Stir until salt dissolves and pour over vegetables.

4. Cover with cling wrap, nick twice and cook 20 minutes, turning dish 4 times. Stand 5 minutes, spoon out on to warm plates and top each with a dollop of cream.

HUNGARY - JEWISH

Tarhonya/Farfel

Serves 6–8
Power Level Full
Cooking Time 8½ minutes

2oz (50g) onion

1oz (25g) lard or margarine

---

1 pack (8.8oz or 250g) toasted farfel

1½ level tsp salt

1¼pt (750ml) boiling water

Tarhonya is Hungarian pasta or Jewish pasta, whichever suits. It is available in packets (I found it fairly easy to come by in large supermarket chains) and is best bought already toasted. It is always called Farfel in Britain, rarely Tarhonya,

but in Hungary is known by both names. The
pasta is served with paprika and goulash dishes.

1. Peel and finely chop onion. Heat lard or
   margarine in a dish for 1½ minutes. Stir in
   onion and cook 2 minutes.

2. Mix in dry farfel, then add salt and water. Stir
   round.

3. Cover with cling wrap, nick twice and cook
   5 minutes. Stand 3 minutes, drain if necessary,
   stir round with a fork and serve.

INDIA

Serves 4–6
Power Level Full
Cooking Time 27 minutes

1lb (450g) lamb fillet, weight AFTER trimming away fat

3 tblsp salad oil

1 garlic clove, peeled and crushed

Seeds from 5 cardamom pods, crushed (use pestle and mortar)

½ level tsp ground ginger

1 level tsp ground cumin

1 level tsp ground coriander

1 level tsp turmeric

½ level tsp ground mace or nutmeg

8oz (225g) American long grain rice

Lamb Biriani

A mild but warmly spiced curry, characteristically dry and usually accompanied by soft chapatis (Indian bread). Serve with condiments of yogurt, sliced onions, lime pickle and sweet mango chutney.

1pt (575ml) hot chicken stock
or water

2 level tsp salt

4oz (125g) flaked and toasted
almonds

Fresh coriander

1. Wash and dry lamb then cut into small cubes, about the same size as dice.

2. Pour oil into a fairly large dish. Heat 2 minutes. Add lamb, garlic and all the spices. Mix thoroughly then arrange mixture round edges, leaving a hollow in the centre.

3. Cover with cling wrap, nick twice and cook 10 minutes. Uncover then stir in rice, stock and salt.

4. Cover as above and cook 15 minutes. Stand 3 minutes, mound on to hot plates and serve very hot. Sprinkle each portion with almonds and coriander leaves.

Serves allow 2 per person
Power Level Full
Cooking Time 45 seconds

1 packet Poppadoms

Poppadoms (Poppadums)

Indian crisps! They can be eaten as an appetiser before an Indian meal or crushed and sprinkled over a curry. Recently the Standard Tandoori restaurant in Acton, West London, presented me with a dish of sliced up, sweet onions to go with the Poppadoms while at Diwana's in North West London, I was given a dish of potent lime pickle. Both were well received.

Place 1 poppadom (6 inches or 15cm) on a flat bread and butter plate. Cook 45 seconds uncovered, turning over once. Leave to cool and crispen while microwaving others.

Vegetable Curry

Serves 6
Power Level Full
Cooking Time 30–35 minutes

4oz (125g) red or green pepper
8oz (225g) carrots
12oz (350g) courgettes
8oz (225g) unpeeled aubergine
12oz (325g) potatoes
6oz (175g) brussels sprouts
6oz (175g) onions
2 tblsp corn or groundnut oil
1 garlic clove
3 slightly rounded tblsp tomato purée
1 level tsp turmeric
3 level tsp garam masala
2 level tsp rogan josh curry powder (mild)
1 level tsp ground coriander
1 level tsp ground cumin
2 to 3 level tsp salt
1 bay leaf
1 can (14oz or 400g) tomatoes
¼pt (150ml) boiling water

A fairly typical vegetarian curry, by Indian standards, with all the vegetables staying a mite crisp and the sauce a warm golden brown. Serve over Patna or brown rice with crushed Poppadoms on top. A side dish of thick yogurt is cooling, although I have kept the curry mild and left you to hot it up yourself with chilli powder or Tabasco.

1. Wash and dry pepper. Cut in half and remove inside fibres and seeds. Finely shred flesh.

2. Peel carrots and courgettes and slice very thinly. (Use a food processor if you have one.)

3. Wash and dry aubergine. Peel potatoes and wash. Cut both into small cubes. Trim and wash sprouts then halve each.

4. Peel onions and cut into very thin slices. Pour

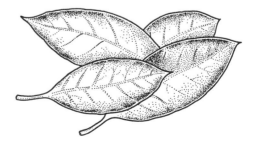

oil into a 5pt (2.75ml litres) dish. Add onions, stir round and cook, uncovered, for 5 minutes.

5. Remove from oven. Peel and slice garlic. Add to dish with all remaining ingredients except water.

6. Mix thoroughly, crushing down tomatoes with a fork. Cover with large inverted plate or matching lid.

7. Cook for 25 to 30 minutes or until vegetables are tender but still firm to the bite. Stir at least 4 times.

8. Mix in the boiling water, remove bay leaf and adjust seasoning to taste – the curry may need a bit of extra salt.

Serves 4
Power Level Full
Cooking Time 13½ minutes

1oz (25g) butter or 4 tsp peanut oil

4oz (125g) onions, peeled and finely chopped

---

2 garlic cloves, peeled and crushed

---

1 level tblsp Madras curry powder

---

1 level tsp ground cummin

---

2 tblsp fresh lime juice

¼pt (150ml) vegetable or fish stock

---

2 level tblsp tomato purée

2oz (50g) sultanas

1lb (450–500g) peeled prawns, thawed completely if frozen

Prawns Madras

From the old days of the Raj is this vibrant fish curry, delicately sweetened with sultanas and bordered with rice. Accompany with Poppadoms (page 78), a dish of cool yogurt mixed with chopped fresh coriander, mango chutney and cut-up tomatoes.

1. Heat butter or oil for 1 minute in an 8-inch (20cm) round dish. Add onions and garlic, stir well and cook, uncovered, for 3 minutes. Mix in curry powder, cummin and lime juice. Leave uncovered and cook 3 minutes, stirring twice.

2. Add stock, purée and sultanas. Cover with an inverted plate and cook 5 minutes.

3. Drain prawns, add to dish and cook, uncovered, for 1½ minutes. Stir round and serve.

Vegetable Madras
Make exactly as above, substituting the same weight of cooked diced vegetables for the prawns. After adding to dish, cover with an inverted plate and cook 3 minutes at full.

INDONESIA

Makes 8 Skewers
Power Level Full
Cooking Time 10 minutes

Pork Satay

A Far Eastern delicacy and a cousin of the Turkish and Balkan kebab. The Satay sauce to accompany is something special and enriched with wholenut peanut butter. Rice is the usual side dish.

Marinade

2 tblsp groundnut oil

2 tblsp soy sauce

1 garlic clove, peeled and crushed

2lb (just under 1kg) fillet of pork

8 wooden skewers

Satay sauce

2 tsp groundnut oil

3oz (75g) onions

2 green chillies

2 garlic cloves

1/4pt (150ml) hot water

4 level tblsp wholenut peanut butter

1. For marinade, pour oil into a bowl. Stir in soy sauce and garlic. Trim fat off pork then cut meat into 1-inch (2.5cm) narrow strips. Add to bowl, mix well and cover. Leave to stand in the kitchen for 4 hours but, when it is very hot outside, refrigerate for 8 hours.

2. Meanwhile, prepare ingredients for Satay sauce. Pour oil into a bowl. Peel and finely chop onions. Wash and dry chillies, slit, de-seed and finely chop. Peel and crush garlic. Add all three to bowl.

3. Before serving, lift pork out of marinade and thread on to the skewers. Arrange 4 skewers on a large plate, as near to the edges as

2 tsp white wine vinegar

Salt and freshly ground black pepper to taste

possible. Cook 5 minutes, turning once. Repeat with remaining skewers. Put both lots together, cover and keep warm.

4. To complete the sauce, cover bowl with cling wrap, nick twice and cook 2 minutes. Mix in remaining ingredients, leave uncovered and cook 3 minutes, stirring once. Stand ½ minute, stir round and serve with the pork.

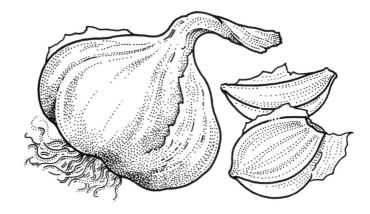

INTERNATIONAL

Creamed Potatoes

Serves 6
Power Level Full
Cooking Time 18 minutes

2lb (1kg) potatoes

6 tblsp boiling water

1 level tblsp salt

1 to 1½oz (25 to 40g) butter or margarine

5 tblsp milk, warm for preference

Totally unsnobby and non-foodie, creamed potatoes are smooth, soft and delicious and the natural companion to all manner of meat, fish, poultry, egg and cheese dishes from Scandinavian meatballs to Britain's shepherd pie. Easily prepared in the microwave, the potatoes can be served in the same dish in which they were cooked, thus saving extra washing up.

1. Peel and wash potatoes then cut into large cubes. Place in fairly deep dish.

2. Add water. Sprinkle with salt, cover with cling wrap, nick twice and cook for 15 minutes, turning dish 4 times.

3. Uncover but don't drain. Mash down thoroughly then work in butter or margarine.

4. Gradually beat in milk until potato mixture is light and creamy. Leave uncovered and reheat until very hot, allowing about 3 minutes.

Duck with Orange Sauce

Serves 4
Power Level Full
Cooking Time 44 minutes

1 duck, about 5lb (2.25kg) in weight

Sauce

Grated peel of 1 medium washed and dried orange

Juice of 2 medium oranges

2 level tblsp fine shred marmalade

1 level tblsp redcurrant jelly

1 to 2 tblsp Grand Marnier or medium sherry

1 tsp soy sauce

2 level tsp cornflour

Trendy always, classy and expensive in restaurants, Duck with Orange Sauce is for celebratory occasions, special times. Now, with the help of the microwave, the complexity of this recipe is reduced to a minimum and can be prepared at home with every confidence.

1. Wash and dry duck then stand on 2 upturned saucers standing in a 12 by 7-inch (30 by 18cm) dish. Cover with cling wrap, nick twice and cook 20 minutes.

2. Drain off fat carefully, turn duck over, cover as above and cook a further 20 minutes. Stand 10 minutes then cut into 4 portions with poultry shears. Keep hot.

3. For sauce, place all ingredients, except cornflour, into a measuring jug and make up to ½pt (275ml) with fat-skimmed duck juices and water if necessary.

4. Mix cornflour with 3 tsp of measured liquid, add to jug and cook 4 minutes, stirring 3 times. Pour over duck and garnish with orange slices and watercress.

Liver Pâté

Serves about 12
Power Level Full
Cooking Time 11 minutes

6oz (175g) butter or margarine

2 garlic cloves, peeled and crushed

1lb (450 to 500g) chicken livers, washed and dried

2 large pinches of nutmeg

White pepper to taste

2 tblsp brandy

Rich, rich, rich; a distinguished liver pâté fit for every memorable occasion. The microwave apart, you will need a blender or food processor to smooth the liver down to a paste-like consistency. On a high fashion note, accompany with a well-chilled sweet white Muscat wine.

1. Cut up butter or margarine, put into a 3pt (1.75 litre) dish and melt for about 3 minutes.

2. Mix in garlic and livers, cover with cling wrap and nick twice. Cook 8 minutes, turning dish 4 times. Stir in nutmeg, pepper and brandy.

3. Work half at a time to a smooth pâté in blender goblet or food processor. Spread into a straight-sided dish, cover with cling wrap and refrigerate until firm. Serve with crisp toast.

Liver Pâté with Orange and Pistachios

A vibrant blend of flavours makes this pâté unusual, colourful and the perfect dinner party starter.

Make as above, using Cointreau instead of brandy. Stir in 2oz (50g) blanched and halved pistachio nuts before spreading into dish.

Roast Chicken

**Serves allow about 8oz (225g) per person
Power Level Full
Cooking Time 8 minutes per 1lb (450g) + 1 minute for melting butter or margarine**

Baste

1oz (25g) butter or margarine

1 level tsp paprika

1 tsp Worcester sauce

1 tsp soy sauce

½ level tsp onion or garlic salt

2 level tsp tomato purée (optional)

Even people who use their microwaves only for de-frosting and re-heating are now discovering the beauty of cooking chicken in their ovens. It *does* brown, provided the bird is well basted beforehand, and what it lacks in crispness is made up for by its superior flavour and moist, succulent flesh. And at only 8 minutes per pound (450 to 500g) cooking time, the saving in energy costs is appreciable. You can still serve it traditionally with Bread Sauce, bacon rolls and small chipolata sausages, but if you want stuffing additionally, cook separately rather than inside the body cavity. This is because the bird would overcook on the outside, leaving the inside raw, tepid and unhealthy – a natural breeding ground for germs.

For the baste, put butter or margarine in a small basin and melt for about 1 minute, uncovered, at full power. Beat in rest of ingredients.

To complete

Place washed and dried chicken, size to suit, in a dish. Brush well with baste. Cover with cling wrap and nick twice. Cook for 8 minutes per lb (450g), turning dish 4 times. Switch off the microwave halfway through and allow bird to stand for 10 minutes before continuing to cook. After cooking, transfer to a carving board, cover with foil and leave to stand 7 minutes.

Bread Sauce

Serves 6
Power Level Full
Cooking Time 5½ minutes

3oz (75g) onion

---

1 bay leaf

---

4 cloves

½pt (275ml) cold milk

---

2 large pinches grated nutmeg

6oz (175g) fresh white breadcrumbs

½oz (15g) butter

---

2 tblsp double cream or extra thick cream

½ to 1 level tsp salt

---

1. Peel onion and cut into quarters. Put into a basin with next 4 ingredients. Leave uncovered and cook 4 minutes, turning dish twice.

2. Remove from oven, cover with a plate and leave to stand for 15 minutes. Strain and pour into a clean bowl.

3. Mix in rest of ingredients. Leave uncovered and cook about 1½ to 2 minutes or until hot. Stir twice and serve.

Carrot Cake

Serves 8
Power Level Full
Cooking Time 6 minutes

Cake

6oz (175g) carrots

1½oz (40g) walnut pieces

2oz (50g) sugar-rolled chopped dates

6oz (175g) light brown soft sugar

Moist, succulent, lightly-spiced, warmly golden brown and packed with walnuts and carrots, this is one of the best microwave cakes I've made in a long time. It uses oil instead of the more conventional butter or margarine and may therefore be eaten by health buffs with a relatively clear conscience, provided they turn a blind eye to the sugar within (though it's brown) and the fairly rich cream cheese topping (removable). Turning to thoughts of Halloween and Guy Fawkes, there is a second version of the

2 eggs (Grade 2), at kitchen temperature

6 fluid oz (175ml) sunflower oil

1 tsp vanilla essence

2 tblsp milk

5oz (150g) plain flour

1 level tsp baking powder

¾ level tsp soda bicarbonate

1 level tsp mixed spice

Topping

6oz (175g) cream cheese, at kitchen temperature

1 tsp vanilla essence

3oz (75g) icing sugar, sifted

3 tsp lemon juice, strained if fresh

cake made with raw pumpkin and dark brown soft sugar, a thing of joy with hot toddy or mugs of foaming chocolate.

1. Brush a plastic ring mould (designed for microwave cooking) lightly with sunflower oil. It should be about 8½ inches (22cm) in diameter tapering to a base measurement of 7½ inches (19cm). The depth should be around 2 inches (5cm). Line base with a circle of non-stick parchment paper.

2. Peel carrots and cut into chunks. Put into a food processor or blender with walnuts and run machine until both are chopped – but not too finely; rather like a coarse paste.

3. Transfer to a bowl and work in dates, sugar, eggs, oil, essence and milk. Sift together dry ingredients. Mix into carrot mixture with a fork.

4. Transfer to mould, cover with cling wrap and nick twice. Cook 6 minutes, turning 3 times. Stand 15 minutes then invert on to a wire

rack. Peel off lining paper and leave until cold. Invert on to a plate.

5. To complete, beat topping ingredients well together and spread over top of cake. Leave until set before cutting.

Halloween Cake
Make as carrot cake, substituting pumpkin flesh for carrots. Use dark brown soft sugar instead of light brown and allspice in place of mixed spice.

Serves 6
Power Level Full and Defrost
Cooking Time 6 minutes

1oz (25g) butter or margarine

2oz (50g) light brown soft sugar

2 level tblsp cocoa powder

2 level tblsp golden syrup

2 tblsp rich milk or single cream

1 tsp vanilla essence

Hot Chocolate Sauce

Nothing could be finer, drizzled over Profiteroles or ice cream.

1. Put butter or margarine into a small bowl, leave uncovered and melt 1 minute at full.

2. Add remaining ingredients and stir well to mix.

3. Leave uncovered and heat until sauce is smooth and hot. Allow 5 minutes at defrost and stir 4 times.

Mocha Sauce
Flavoured with coffee, this is a superb sauce for ice cream sundaes.

Make as above, adding 2 rounded tsp coffee granules with remaining ingredients.

ISRAEL

Serves 4–5
Power Level Full
Cooking Time 10 minutes

1½pt (900ml) clear chicken
soup (the real thing if
possible, otherwise chicken
stock cubes in hot water)

1 large, ripe avocado

2 tblsp lemon juice

Chicken and Avocado Soup

With avocados becoming as popular in Israel as
they are everywhere else, this is a contemporary
soup by local standards, different from the clear
soups and heavy broths brought to this patch in
the Middle East from all over the world. It's very
uncomplicated to make and useful if you want a
light starter with a bit of warmth to it.

1. Pour soup into a bowl. Cover with an
   inverted plate and heat for 9 minutes.

2. Meanwhile, mash avocado with lemon juice.
   Add to soup. Re-cover and heat a further
   minute. Stir round and serve.

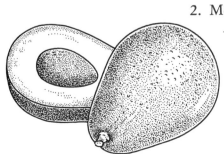

91

ITALY

Serves 4
Power Level
Defrost and Full
Cooking Time 12 minutes

4oz (125g) frozen chopped spinach
2oz (50g) butter or margarine, at kitchen temperature
2oz (50g) semolina
1 egg (Grade 3), beaten
½ level tsp salt
¼ level tsp grated nutmeg
¼pt (150ml) milk
2oz (50g) grated Emmental cheese
2 heaped tsp grated Parmesan cheese

Baby Spinach Gnocchi

Pronounced 'nockie', these are small semolina dumplings from Italy, coloured green and flavoured with spinach. Poached in milk and served with a cheese flavoured sauce, they make an appetising meal starter which is also economical.

1. Place spinach in a shallow dish, leave uncovered and cook for 3 minutes at defrost. Tip into a mesh sieve and press out liquid with the back of a spoon – spinach should be as dry as possible. Return to dish and cook a further 2 minutes at defrost.

2. Put butter or margarine into a bowl and beat until light in colour and texture. Gradually work in semolina, egg, salt, nutmeg and spinach. Cover and refrigerate for 1½ to 2 hours.

3. Using floured hands, shape mixture into 16 lozenge shapes, each 2 inches (5cm) in length.

4. Pour milk into a 7-inch (18cm) round and shallow dish, leave uncovered and heat for 2 minutes at full power. Place 8 gnocchi round edge of dish and cook for 2 minutes at full power, turning over once with a spoon.

5. Lift out of dish and transfer to a warm plate. Cook rest of gnocchi in the same way and add to plate.

6. To complete, mix Emmental cheese with milk in dish and heat until melted, allowing about 1 minute at full power. Pour over gnocchi, sprinkle with Parmesan cheese and eat hot.

Neapolitan Sauce

Serves 4
Power Level Full
Cooking Time 6 minutes

1 pack (500g) strained mashed tomatoes (available from supermarket chains)

2 tsp olive or corn oil

2 garlic cloves, peeled and crushed (or use 1 if preferred)

2 tsp granulated sugar

1 level tsp dried basil

1 level tsp salt

Pasta (Pages 95–6)

8oz (225g) pasta such as spaghetti, lasagne, shells, macaroni

A speedy compromise between old and new, this is a zesty pasta sauce which is ready in 6 minutes.

1. Place all ingredients together in a deepish bowl and stir well to mix.

2. Cover with cling wrap, nick twice and cook 6 minutes. Stir and serve over any pasta to taste.

Pasta
To cook in dry form from a packet (for 4 servings)
Place 8oz (225g) pasta of any kind you like into a dish, snapping long spaghetti into shortish lengths. Add 1½pt (850ml) boiling water, 1 to 1½ level tsp salt, 2 tsp salad oil. Cook, uncovered, for 10 to 15 minutes or until 'al dente' – soft but still a little bit chewy – stirring 4 times. Don't be tempted to overcook as the pasta will become soggy. Stir round, cover with an inverted plate and leave to stand 5 minutes. Drain and use as required.

To cook small dry pasta such as vermicelli, and alphabets (for 4 servings)
Follow directions in above recipe but cook only for 8 to 10 minutes. Stand 3 minutes, covered. Drain and use as required.

To cook fresh pasta – home made or bought in packets (for 4 servings)
Follow first recipe, but use only 1pt (575ml) boiling water to 8oz (225g) pasta. Cook for half the time of dry pasta. Cover, stand 3 or 4 minutes, drain and serve.

Serves 4
Power Level Full
Cooking Time
1–1½ minutes

---

8 oz (225g) raw weight of freshly cooked spaghetti (see recipes following)

---

1 egg yolk

¼pt (150ml) double cream

---

2 to 3 level tblsp finely grated Parmesan cheese

---

8 medium sized spring onions, trimmed and chopped

Seasoning to taste

Pasta Crema

Speckled with chopped spring onions and nestling in Parmesan cheese and cream, this is Italian cuisine at its most classic – a simple pleasure that goes hand in hand with a lively mixed salad in a dressing based on olive oil. In the gourmet class and especially for vegetarians.

1. Drain spaghetti thoroughly and return to dish.

2. Beat together egg yolk, cream, cheese and onions. Add to spaghetti and toss well to mix.

3. Leave uncovered and reheat until hot, allowing about 1 to 1½ minutes. Stand 2 minutes, stir round and serve. Pass extra Parmesan cheese separately for sprinkling over the top of each portion.

95

Ragú Sauce (Bolognese)

Serves 4
Power Level Full
Cooking Time 21 minutes

4oz (125g) onions
4oz (125g) carrots
2oz (50g) celery
3oz (75g) mushrooms
2 tblsp olive or corn oil
2 garlic cloves
12oz (350g) lean minced beef
1 can (14oz or 400g) tomatoes in tomato juice
2 level tblsp tomato purée
¼pt (150ml) dryish red wine
1 level tsp sugar
1 to 1½ level tsp salt

THE pasta sauce, a feast for every Italian, used almost daily and perhaps better known as the Bolognese. Ours by nationwide adoption, the sauce works like a charm in the microwave. If preferred, substitute water or beef stock for the wine.

1. Peel onions and carrots then finely chop. Wash and scrub celery and cut into narrow strips. Trim mushrooms and thinly slice.

2. Pour oil into a 2pt (1¼ litre) dish. Add prepared vegetables and stir round until well-mixed. Leave uncovered and cook 6 minutes, stirring once or twice and turning dish 3 or 4 times.

3. Peel garlic and crush into dish. Add beef and tomatoes and gently squash down both so that they are well mixed with the other ingredients.

4. Add purée, wine and sugar and mix in thoroughly. Cover dish with cling wrap, nick twice and cook 15 minutes, turning dish twice. Stand 5 minutes, season with salt, stir round and serve.

Above: Roast Leg of Pork with Crackling (p 53)
Boned and Rolled Roast Joint (p 54)
Roast Chicken (p 87)
(Photo: Paxo)
Below: Christmas Pudding (p 56)
(Photo: McDougall's Flour)

Overleaf, above: Cod in Cider Sauce (p 39)
(Photo: The Butter Information Council)
Overleaf, below: Plum Crumble (p 58)
(Photo: McDougall's Flour)

JAPAN

Serves 3–4
Power Level Full
Cooking Time 11 minutes

9oz (250g) cooked chicken

4 fluid oz (100ml) hot chicken
or beef stock

4 tblsp medium sherry

2 tblsp soy sauce

3 tsp light brown soft sugar

4 eggs (Grade 2), well beaten

Chicken with Eggs

Food exquisitely presented with artistry and elegance, the Japanese are known for their decorative talents and use these skills to produce plate arrangements which are highly ornate, delicate and immensely edible. Chicken with Eggs is a departure from tradition and, though not particularly beautiful, is a practical family dish and a unique way of using up leftovers. Plenty of rice is called for.

1. Cut chicken into strips and leave aside temporarily. Pour next 3 ingredients into a shallow 7-inch (18cm) round dish. Stir in sugar, cover with cling wrap, nick twice and cook for 5 minutes. Stir round.

2. Mix in chicken. Pour beaten eggs over the top, leave uncovered and cook for 6 minutes, turning dish 3 times.

3. Spoon hot rice into bowls and top with chicken and egg mixture.

JEWISH

Serves 4 as a Starter, 6 as an
Appetiser
Power Level Defrost
Cooking Time 11½ minutes

1½oz (40g) margarine
(vegetable only)

4 eggs (Grade 1 or jumbo-
size)

1½oz (40g) onion

Salt and pepper to taste

Chopped Egg and Onion

Classically Jewish, the egg mixture may be
served as a meal starter with matzos (unleavened
bread) (page 99), or spread on to biscuits and
offered round as appetisers. The main advantage
of microwaving the eggs is to save washing up
(they cook in a cup) and also cut down on
energy costs and a steamy kitchen.

1. Put margarine into a cup, leave uncovered and
   cook for 2½ minutes. Leave aside.

2. Line a breakfast cup with cling wrap. Break in
   eggs, puncture yolks with fork and cover cup
   with a saucer. Cook 5 minutes, stand
   4 minutes then cook an extra 4 minutes. Cool
   in the cup till almost cold.

3. Peel and chop onions on a board and put into
   a mixing bowl. Tip eggs out on to the same
   board and finely chop.

4. Add to onions with melted margarine. Mix thoroughly and season to taste with salt and pepper. Mound on to 4 bread and butter plates and serve as a starter. Alternatively, use to cover small biscuits for appetisers.

Note

As Jewish people are not allowed to eat dairy foods with meat, it is essential to use vegetable margarine for the Egg and Onion unless the main course is fish or a cheese dish.

Matzo Balls (Kneidlech)

Serves 6–8
Power Level Full
Cooking Time 8 minutes

4oz (125g) medium matzo meal

¼ level tsp salt

½ level tsp onion salt

1 tblsp margarine (healthier than the more usual liquid chicken fat)

8 fluid oz (225ml) boiling water

1 egg (Grade 1)

Made from the meal of unleavened bread (matzos), these are known to every Jewish family worldwide. They are traditionally served in the Sabbath chicken soup (clear broth) and are tasty dumplings from the Old World. The matzo meal is available from large supermarket chains.

1. Tip matzo meal into a fairly large bowl. Toss in both salts.

2. Add margarine and boiling water then stir well to make a thick, puddingy mixture.

3. Beat in egg thoroughly, cover bowl and refrigerate for 1 hour. Shape into 18 small balls.

4. Return to washed and dried bowl, top up

with boiling water and stand on a plate in case water boils over.

5. Cover with cling wrap, nick twice and cook for 8 minutes. Drain and add to hot soup.

Tip
To heat and cook the matzo balls and soup together, pour soup into a large bowl, cover with plate and cook for 10 minutes on full power. Add balls, cover as before and cook 8 minutes. Ladle directly into plates.

Serves 6–8

Matzo Balls with Syrup
A variation from me. Omit onion salt from matzo mixture. Cook balls as directed above. Leave in water. Melt 5oz (150g) golden syrup in a bowl for 3 minutes at defrost setting. Leave uncovered. Drain matzo balls, put on to pudding plates and coat with syrup.

Makes 20
Power Level Defrost
Cooking Time 8 minutes

2 egg whites (Grade 2)

4oz (125g) caster sugar

1½ level tblsp cinnamon

8oz (225g) ground almonds

Sifted icing sugar

Cinnamon Balls for Passover

Passover is a holiday festival in the spring which often coincides with Easter and celebrates the liberation of the Jewish people from their bondage in Egypt. It is the season of unleavened bread called matzos (history tells us there was no time for fleeing Jews to wait for bread to rise) which look like long square crackers packed into boxes, biscuits laden with almonds and skyscraper cakes made from eggs, sugar and fine matzo meal; wheat flour is never used by the Orthodox during Passover week. The Cinnamon Balls below are traditional festival biscuits with soft and moist centres, the outsides coated liberally with icing sugar. They are quite delicious, expensive to make, more so to buy and work to perfection in the microwave. Do try.

1. Beat egg whites until just foamy then work in sugar, cinnamon and almonds.

2. Roll into 20 balls with wetted hands. Put on to the edge of a dinner plate in 2 rings.

3. Leave uncovered and cook 8 minutes, turning plate 4 times. Cool to lukewarm and roll in icing sugar until each one is heavily coated.

4. Store airtight when completely cool.

Continental Cheese Cake

Serves 8
Power Level Defrost
Cooking Time 15 minutes

3oz (75g) digestive biscuits, crushed

1lb (450 to 500g) curd cheese, at kitchen temperature

---

3 eggs (Grade 1), at kitchen temperature

Finely grated peel and juice of 1 washed and dried lemon

3oz (75g) caster sugar

2oz (50g) seedless raisins

---

1 carton (5oz or 142ml) soured cream

An Old World cheesecake which was brought to this country by turn of the century Jewish emigrées from North, Central and Eastern Europe. It is uncomplicated as cheesecakes go, with a slight tang and creamy texture.

1. Well grease a glass pie plate with a top measurement of 8½ inches (21cm) in diameter, sloping to a base measurement of 7 inches (18cm). Cover base with biscuits.

2. Put cheese into a bowl and beat in eggs, grated lemon peel and juice, sugar and raisins.

3. Pour into pie plate over crumbs and cook for 15 minutes, turning 4 times.

4. Remove from oven and spread top with the soured cream. Cool and refrigerate until firm.

Tip
For a special sweet, top portions of the cheesecake with Cranberry Sauce (page 118) and the Dutch Blender Cream (page 106).

MIDDLE EAST - BALKANS

Serves 4–6
Power Level Full
Cooking Time 8–10 minutes

1 medium aubergine, about 1lb or 450g

2 level tblsp tahini (sesame seed paste in jars from most supermarkets)

2 tblsp freshly squeezed lemon juice, strained

2 spring onions, trimmed and finely chopped

2 heaped tblsp chopped fresh coriander

1 garlic clove, peeled and crushed

1 level tsp salt

2 pinches of sugar

Pepper to taste

Aubergine Dip

A happy arrangement of flavours and a pleasurable dip to serve cold with warm pitta and sesame seed bread. Also black olives.

1. Wash aubergine, top and tail then prick skin all over with a fork. Transfer to a plate and cook 8 to 10 minutes or until it feels very soft to the touch. Turn over once and keep your hand protected by an oven glove.

2. Cool down, cut in half and scoop flesh into a bowl. Mash down as finely as possible then work in rest of ingredients.

MIDDLE EAST

Shredded Dessert with Pistachios

Serves 8–10
Power Level Full
Cooking Time 7½ minutes

4oz (125g) pistachio nuts
(bright green when peeled)

6 shredded wheats (breakfast
cereal)

4oz (125g) caster sugar

¼pt (150ml) milk

2oz (50g) butter (use
margarine as a compromise)

3 tblsp orange flower water
(order in advance from a
pharmacy)

Fragrant with orange flower water and chopped pistachios, this is the book's pièce de résistance, a wonderful dessert, costly I accept because of the nuts, but a treasure to keep up your sleeve for special entertaining. Accompany, if you can, with little cups of strong Turkish style coffee as indeed one would expect in parts of the Middle East. Alternatively, make Espresso if you have a suitable machine.

1. Cover nuts with boiling water. Leave to stand a few minutes then drain and slide off skins. Chop fairly finely.

2. Butter an 8-inch (20cm) round dish and crumble 3 shredded wheats across the base.

3. Mix together nuts and sugar then sprinkle evenly over the shredded wheat in dish.

Crumble remaining shredded wheat and spread evenly over nuts and sugar.

4. Heat milk and butter, uncovered, for 1½ minutes. Add orange flower water and spoon gently over dessert.

5. Leave uncovered and cook for 6 minutes. Serve hot or at room temperature.

Dried Fruit Salad

Serves 4
Power Level Medium and Full
Cooking Time 11 minutes

1 packet (250g or 9oz approximately) dried fruit salad

½pt (275ml) boiling water

3oz (75g) caster sugar

2 tblsp lemon juice

¼pt (150ml) extra hot water

1 tblsp orange flower or rose water (available from pharmacies)

Full of fragrance and enhanced with either orange flower water or rose water, this fruit salad is a favourite in the Middle East where it is served cold with cream and a sprinkle of chopped walnuts, almonds or pistachios.

1. Wash fruit well, put into a glass basin and add boiling water. Cover with an inverted plate and cook on medium for 5 minutes.

2. Remove from oven and soak 3 hours. Return to oven, add sugar, lemon juice and rest of hot water. Cover as before.

3. Cook at full power for 6 minutes, stirring twice. Cool to lukewarm then mix in the flower water. Cover and refrigerate until cold before serving.

THE
NETHERLANDS

Serves 4–6
Power Level Full
Cooking Time 2½ minutes

¼pt (150ml) full cream milk

5oz (150g) Dutch unsalted butter, from the refrigerator

Dutch Blender Cream

Imagine, cream almost while you wait and no last minute chase to the corner shop because it was missed off the shopping list. I like this one very much. It can be whipped like ordinary whipping cream and has a soft, smooth and snow-like texture. It is meant for hot apple pie and summer strawberries.

1. Pour milk into a bowl. Cut in pieces of butter.

2. Leave uncovered and heat through for 2½ minutes.

3. Blend for 60 seconds in a blender, return to bowl and chill in the refrigerator for 2 to 3 hours.

4. Stir round and pour over puddings. If preferred, whip first.

NEW ZEALAND

Serves 10
Power Level Defrost
Cooking Time 6–7 minutes

Crust

6oz (175g) butter or margarine

4oz (125g) soft brown sugar

8oz (225g) crushed malt biscuits or digestives

Filling

12oz (350g) tamarillos (4 pieces of fruit)

Boiling water

4oz (125g) light brown soft sugar

6 level tsp or 1½ pkts powder gelatine

2 fluid oz (50ml) cold water

Tamarillo Cheesecake

Surprise, surprise from a friendly lady in Christchurch, New Zealand. Reading my comments on Tamarillos in a magazine – I said they were expensive over here, which they are – Beverley Blair wrote back saying 'used in a cheesecake which is extravagant to start with, one can justify the expense as a special treat'. She's right, of course, and this is how I've adapted her recipe with a fruit, native to Peru and cultivated in New Zealand, which closely resembles the tomato. I much appreciate her kindness in bothering to write to me at all and for her luscious cake, 'cooked' in the refrigerator.

1. Well-rinse a 10-inch (25cm) metal spring clip tin and leave sides undried.

2. For crust, put butter or margarine into a large bowl, leave uncovered and melt at defrost

107

10oz (275g) cream cheese

3 eggs (Grade 2), separated

Juice of ½ lemon

setting for 3 minutes. Stir in sugar and biscuits then spread fairly thickly over base of tin. Refrigerate while making cake.

3. Put tamarillos into a bowl, cover with the boiling water to loosen skin. Drain, peel (like tomatoes) and slice. Sprinkle with half the sugar.

4. Put gelatine into another small bowl. Stir in the cold water and soften for 3 to 4 minutes. Leave uncovered and melt in microwave for 3 to 4 minutes.

5. Stir round and return to microwave for a further minute or so if undissolved particles are still visible.

6. Put cheese into a bowl. Gradually beat in warm gelatine mixture, egg yolks, lemon juice and rest of sugar.

7. Stiffly whisk egg whites and fold into cheese with the tamarillos. Spoon into the tin over biscuit base and refrigerate overnight.

POLAND

Serves 4
Power Level Full
Cooking Time 5½ minutes

1lb (450 to 500g) mushrooms

1oz (25g) butter

1 level tblsp flour

1 carton (5oz or 142ml) soured cream

½ level tsp salt

Mushrooms with Cream

Highly-prized by all Polish people are mushrooms, a grand feast at all times and often served as a main course with boiled potatoes.

1. Trim mushrooms, wipe and slice.

2. Put butter into a bowl, leave uncovered and melt 1 minute. Stir in mushrooms, cover with an inverted plate and cook 2 minutes.

3. Mix in flour and cream. Cover as above and cook 2½ minutes. Stir round, season with salt and serve with hot boiled potatoes.

Compôte of Pears in Wine with Rum

Serves 4
Power Level Full
Cooking Time 12 minutes

¼pt (150ml) red wine

4oz (125g) granulated sugar

4 medium-sized firm dessert pears, Williams or Comice for preference

Strained juice of 1 large lemon

2 tblsp dark rum

Poland is noted for superb ice creams and equally lavish desserts – this is one of them and should be served with softly-whipped and lightly-sweetened cream dusted with cinnamon.

1. Pour wine into an 8-inch (20cm) round dish by about 3-inch (8cm) in depth.

2. Add sugar. Leave uncovered and cook for 4 minutes, stirring twice.

3. Peel, halve and core pears, taking care not to break through the flesh. Arrange in dish with the pointed ends of each half placed towards the centre.

4. Cover with an inverted plate and cook 4 minutes. Turn pears over, cover again and cook a further 4 minutes.

5. Stir in lemon juice and leave to cool. Add rum and refrigerate until well-chilled before serving.

PORTUGAL

Serves 4
Power Level Full
Cooking Time 23–23¼ minutes

1oz (25g) butter or margarine or 1½ tblsp olive oil

2 medium onions (4oz or 125g to 250g), peeled and quartered

2 garlic cloves, peeled and crushed

2lb (1kg) chicken joints, skinned

4oz (125g) cooked gammon, cut into small cubes

½lb (225g) tomatoes, blanched, skinned and chopped

¼pt (150ml) dry white wine

2 level tsp mild French mustard

1 to 1½ level tsp salt

Chicken Casserole

Full-flavoured and ideally teamed with whole boiled potatoes, a simple casserole with chicken, ham and vegetables makes an attractive mid-week main course and this stylish contribution from Portugal is no exception.

1. Put butter, margarine or oil into an 8-inch (20cm) round dish and heat until hot, allowing about 1 to 1¼ minutes.

2. Stir in onions and garlic. Leave uncovered and cook 3 minutes. Wash and dry chicken, add to dish, cover with cling wrap and nick twice.

3. Cook 14 minutes, turning dish twice. Stir in gammon, tomatoes, wine, mustard and salt. Cover as above and cook a further 5 minutes. Stand 5 minutes before serving.

ROMANIA

Polenta with Eggs and Cream

Serves 4
Power Level Full
Cooking Time 5 minutes

1¼pt (750ml) boiling water

1½ level tsp salt

7oz (200g) polenta (yellow cornmeal)

2oz (50g) butter or margarine

Topping

8 freshly poached eggs, still hot

2oz (50g) melted butter, still hot

1 carton (5oz or 142ml) soured cream

Mention Polenta to any Romanian, anywhere, and his eyes will mist over with nostalgia and his face light up with sudden happiness, for this is the national dish of the country and a force to be reckoned with. Known as Mammaleega or Mammaleiger (the Romanian spelling is quite different and not readily understood or identifiable by foreigners), this is thick cornmeal cooked with water and butter, topped with freshly poached eggs, coated with melted butter and mounded with spoons of soured cream. To say it is rich is understating the whole situation. It is inordinately rich, lavish, quite one of the most classy non-meat dishes in the world.

1. Pour water into a fairly deep dish. Add salt, polenta and butter or margarine. Leave uncovered and cook 5 minutes until thick, stirring 3 or 4 times.

2. Mound on to 4 warm plates. Make dips in the centre of each, fill with eggs, coat with butter and gently top with soured cream (left to warm up to room temperature first).

RUSSIA

Serves 6
Power Level Full
Cooking Time 35 minutes

1lb (450 to 500g) raw beetroots
5 tblsp water
3oz (75g) carrots
2oz (50g) turnip
3oz (75g) onions
1¼pt (750ml) boiling beef stock
4oz (125g) white cabbage, shredded
1 tblsp lemon juice
½ to 1 level tsp salt

Bortsch

A Russian institution and favoured by all Eastern Europe countries, this characteristically deep red beetroot and cabbage soup is a warming winter happiness, topped with soured cream or thick, Greek yogurt.

1. Wash beetroots thoroughly, leave unpeeled and put into a dish with water. Cover with cling wrap, nick twice and cook 15 minutes.

2. Meanwhile, peel carrots, turnip and onions then grate fairly finely. Transfer to a large bowl. Peel and slice beets and add to bowl with ¼pt (150ml) of the measured stock. Cover as above and cook 10 minutes.

3. Mix in rest of stock, cabbage, lemon juice and salt. Cover with an inverted plate and cook 10 minutes, stirring 3 or 4 times.

4. Ladle soup into warm bowls and top each with soured cream or yogurt. Serve while still hot.

Vegetarian Bortsch
Use vegetable stock instead of beef.

Bortsch at Speed

Serves 4
Power Level Full
Cooking Time 8 minutes

---

1 can consommé (use double strength Campbells)

½pt (275ml) boiling water

¼ level tsp garlic powder

---

1 tblsp lemon juice

6oz (175g) baby pickled beetroots in a jar, drained and sliced

---

2 tblsp pickling vinegar (from jar)

Snappily swift, brightly-coloured and temptingly flavoured is my simplified version of Russia's beetroot soup. Add a traditional boiled potato to each portion plus a dollop of soured cream and a frond of dill. Pretty for entertaining.

1. Put all ingredients into a deepish bowl and cover with an inverted plate.

2. Cook 7 minutes. Strain. Reheat 1 minute and serve as suggested above.

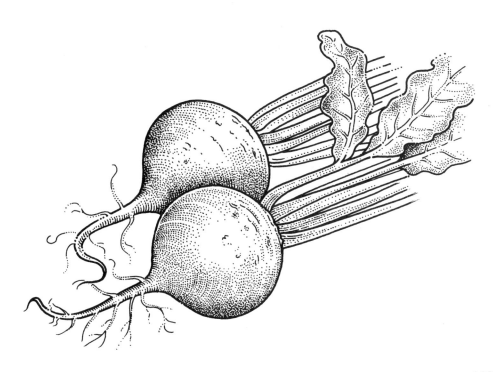

115

Kissel

Serves 4
Power Level Full
Cooking Time 7–7½ minutes

1lb (450 to 500g) mixed berries

4 tblsp red wine, water or apple juice

3oz (75g) caster sugar

½ to 1 tsp vanilla essence

Strips of peel from 1 washed and dried lemon

1 level tblsp arrowroot or cornflour

2 tblsp cold water

More refreshing than almost anything else on a hot summer's day, Kissel is a fruit dessert which sets like a blancmange and is made from freshly gathered berries grown in woods, hedgerows and gardens attached to summer houses in the country.

1. Wash fruit and purée in a food processor or blender goblet. Rub through a fine mesh sieve to remove seeds.

2. Pour wine, water or apple juice into a bowl. Add sugar, essence and lemon peel. Cover with an inverted plate and cook 3 minutes, stirring twice to make sure sugar has dissolved.

3. Add fruit purée, cover as before and cook 2 minutes. Strain, returning mixture to a clean bowl.

4. Blend arrowroot smoothly with water. Add to fruit mixture and cook, uncovered, until thickened. Allow about 2 to 2½ minutes, stirring twice.

5. Pour into 4 dessert dishes, leave until cold then chill in the refrigerator. If liked, float single cream over the top of each.

SCANDINAVIA

Serves 4
Power Level Defrost
Cooking Time 5 minutes

3oz (75g) dried apple rings

¼pt (150ml) cold water

3 rollmop herrings with
onions

¼pt (150ml) whipping cream
or 4 tblsp cream and 4 tblsp
thick Greek yogurt

Rollmop Salad with Apples

Piquant and rich, this salad makes an easy starter when arranged on lettuce-lined plates and accompanied by crispbreads – the thin sort from Sweden.

1. Wash apple rings, break into chunks, put into a bowl and add cold water. Top with an inverted plate. Heat through 5 minutes. Stand 5 minutes then drain.

2. Undo rollmops, removing sticks. Cut into strips and add to apples with onions and cream by itself or cream with yogurt. Mix well.

3. Cover and leave to mature overnight in the refrigerator. Stir round and serve.

Cranberry Sauce

Serves 6
Power Level Full
Cooking Time 8½ minutes

8oz (225g) cranberries,
thawed if frozen

¼pt (150ml) boiling water

6oz (175g) caster sugar

Crisp, bouncy and vivid red, cranberries quickly set with sugar and water into a jellied sauce for game, goose, meatballs, turkey and tongue. This sauce is also popular in North Europe and the USA. Finland uses them to produce one of the richest sweets on earth; a kind of moussey parfait made from stewed berries, whipped cream and egg whites (page 122).

1. Put all ingredients into a deepish dish. Cover with cling wrap and nick twice.

2. Cook 8½ minutes, turning dish 4 times. Serve hot, warm or cold.

Cardamom Cake

Serves 8
Power Level Full
Cooking Time 4 minutes

6oz (175g) self raising flour

½ level tsp baking powder

3oz (75g) butter or margarine

3oz (75g) light brown soft
sugar

1½ level tsp ground
cardamom

---

1 egg (Grade 3)

Cardamom finds its way into many Scandinavian cakes, giving them a subtle flavour and an exotic scent. Most are yeasted but this one is quicker to make and not in the least complicated.

1. Line a 6½-inch (16cm) round dish with cling wrap. The depth should be about 3 inches (8cm).

Cold milk
Topping
½oz (15g) flaked and toasted almonds
1 slightly rounded tblsp soft brown sugar
1 level tsp cinnamon

2. Sift flour and baking powder into a bowl. Rub in butter or margarine then toss in sugar and cardamom.

3. Beat egg in a measuring cup and make up to ¼pt (150ml) with milk. Fork into dry ingredients and mix thoroughly.

4. Pour into dish. Combine topping ingredients and sprinkle over cake.

5. Cover loosely with cling wrap and nick twice. Cook for 4 minutes then leave to stand 5 minutes before turning out on to a wire cooling rack to cool. Reverse before serving so that topping is uppermost.

DENMARK

Serves 6–8
Power Level Full
Cooking Time 45 minutes

2lb (1kg) red cabbage

¾pt (425ml) boiling water

2 level tsp salt

8oz (225g) peeled cooking apples, cored and chopped

8oz (225g) onions, peeled and chopped

2 level tblsp dark brown soft sugar

1 bouquet garni bag

1 bay leaf

1 level tsp caraway seeds

2 level tblsp cornflour

3 tblsp malt vinegar

Red Cabbage with Apples

For pork, for goose, for gammon and duck; a sweet-sour, almost burgundy-red cabbage dish which is part and parcel of a North European and Scandinavian Christmas. For maturity of flavour, the cabbage should be prepared at least one day ahead of time and reheated before eating.

1. Trim cabbage, wash well and finely shred, removing stalky pieces. Transfer to a 4pt (2.25 litre) deep dish and add ½pt (225ml) water and the salt. Mix well, tossing ingredients gently with 2 spoons.

2. Cover with an inverted plate and cook 10 minutes. Stand 5 minutes then mix in all remaining ingredients except the last two. Cover as before and cook 25 minutes, turning dish 4 times. Stand 7 minutes.

120

3. Mix cornflour smoothly with vinegar. Add to cabbage mixture and stir in thoroughly. Cover as before and cook 10 more minutes, stirring 3 times.

4. Remove from oven and refrigerate when cold. Reheat 5 to 8 minutes before serving.

FINLAND

Serves 6

Cranberry Sauce (see page 118)

½pt (275ml) whipping cream

2 egg whites

Cranberry Parfait

Make Cranberry Sauce as on page 118 and completely cool. Beat ½pt (275ml) whipping cream until thick. Whisk 2 egg whites until stiff. Fold cranberry sauce into the cream alternately with egg white. Place in 6 small glasses or dishes and chill lightly before serving.

SWEDEN

Serves 6-8
Power Level Full
Cooking Time 53–54
minutes

12oz (350g) yellow split peas

1½pt (900ml) cold water

1 level tsp marjoram

1 ham bone, weighing about 1lb (450 to 500g)

1¼pt (750ml) extra hot water

2 to 3 level tsp salt

Yellow Pea Soup

Centuries old, this Yellow Pea Soup is Sweden's Thursday Child, eaten once a week in winter for supper followed by pancakes with jam. I was told recently it is customary to drink hot Punch with the soup, the Punch in this case being a Swedish alcoholic drink based on rum. Heady stuff. As a substitute, try rum and hot water with a dash of sugar.

1. Wash peas and put into a bowl. Mix in first amount of water then cover with an inverted plate and heat for 6 minutes. Remove from oven and leave to stand 3 hours.

2. Tip peas and water into a larger bowl. Stir in marjoram then add ham bone.

3. Cover with cling wrap, nick twice and cook for 30 minutes. Mix in half of remaining water. Re-cover as above and cook a further 15 minutes.

4. Take bone out of soup, remove any meat and

cut into small pieces. Return to soup with rest of water and salt. Microwave a further 2 to 3 minutes. Stir round and serve.

Tip

If too thick for personal taste, thin down with boiling water and increase salt to taste.

Cod with White Sauce

Serves 4
Power Level Full
Cooking Time 30–31 minutes

½pt (275ml) cold water
3 cloves
4 juniper berries
1 bay leaf
3oz (75g) onion
2 level tsp salt
4 cod steaks, each 8 to 12oz (225 to 350g)
White Sauce
1oz (25g) butter or margarine
1oz (25g) plain flour
¼pt (150ml) fish liquor, strained
¼pt (150ml) cold milk
Salt and pepper to taste

Devoted to fish as most Scandinavians are, and with fresh catches round the coastline on their doorstep, the accepted rule is to keep the recipes simple so that the delicate flavour of the fish comes through. Swedish cod is a fish lover's fantasy and is usually served with white sauce or melted butter to which one or two chopped hardboiled eggs have been added. Boiled potatoes accompany.

1. For fish, pour water into a measuring jug then add cloves, juniper berries and bay leaf.

2. Peel onion and cut into quarters. Add to jug with salt. Cover with cling wrap, nick twice and cook 15 minutes. Strain.

3. Wash fish and wipe dry with paper towels. Transfer to a 10-inch (25cm) dish. Pour in strained onion liquor, cover with cling wrap, nick twice and cook 10 minutes, turning dish 3 times.

4. Using a fish slice, lift cod out of dish and place on a warm serving plate. Keep hot.

5. For sauce, put butter or margarine into a basin. Melt 1 minute. Stir in flour and cook, uncovered, for a further minute.

6. Gradually blend in warm fish liquor and milk. Cook 4 to 5 minutes or until thickened, stirring after every minute. Season with salt and pepper and serve with the fish.

Serves 4
Power Level Full
Cooking Time 8 minutes to
cook + time for heating up
browning dish; about 10
minutes

---

*3oz (75g) fresh breadcrumbs,
brown or white*

---

*3oz (75g) onions, peeled and
grated*

8oz (225g) minced pork

8oz (225g) minced beef

---

1 large egg

1½ level tsp salt

---

1 small can evaporated milk

¼ to ½ level tsp allspice

1oz (25g) margarine

Köttbullar

One of Sweden's national dishes, these are
nothing more elaborate than spicy meatballs
eaten with boiled potatoes, cranberry sauce and a
green salad. For success, you will need a
browning dish.

1. Combine all ingredients thoroughly and
   shape into 12 even-sized balls. Refrigerate
   until ready to cook.

2. Heat browning dish as directed (instructions
   should be with dish or included in your own
   microwave cook book).

3. Add margarine and swirl it round until base
   of dish is covered. At this stage it will also
   sizzle. Add meatballs and turn over to brown
   both sides.

4. Cover with cling wrap, nick twice and cook
   8 minutes, turning dish 4 times. Stand
   3 minutes before serving.

SPAIN

Paella

Serves 6
Power Level Full
Cooking Time 47 minutes

2lb (1kg) chicken breast
6oz (175g) onions
2 garlic cloves
4oz (125g) green pepper
2 tblsp olive or corn oil
8oz (225g) long grain rice
1 packet saffron strands
6oz (175g) frozen peas (or cooked fresh peas)
8oz (225g) tomatoes, skinned and blanched
1 can (about 8oz or 250g) mussels in brine
3oz (75g) cooked ham, cut into cubes
4oz (125g) peeled prawns

Famous throughout Europe, Paella is a partnership between chicken and shellfish interspersed with saffron rice and peas. It is related to Italy's Risotto and Middle Eastern Pilaf (also spelled Pilaff and Pilav).

1. Put chicken into a 10-inch (25cm) dish, arranging it round edges. Cover with cling wrap, nick twice and cook 15 minutes, turning twice. Drain off liquid and reserve. Cut chicken into small cubes. Wash and dry dish.

2. Peel and chop onions. Peel and crush garlic. Wash and dry pepper and coarsely chop. Pour oil into same dish used for chicken, leave uncovered and heat 1 minute. Stir in onions, garlic and pepper. Leave uncovered and cook 4 minutes.

3. Add all remaining ingredients, including

1pt (575ml) boiling water
1 to 2 level tsp salt
Garnish
Cooked mussels, cooked whole prawns and lemon sliced for garnish

chicken and reserved chicken liquor, but exclude mussels, whole prawns and lemon slices.

4. Cover as above with cling wrap and cook 20 minutes. Stand inside oven for 10 minutes. Continue to cook an extra 7 minutes. Uncover and garnish as in the photograph.

Opposite, above: Fast Moussaka (p 66)
(Photo: Yeoman Instant Mashed Potato)
Opposite, below: Paella (p 127)
(Photo: Uncle Ben's Rice)

Overleaf: Liver Pâté (p 86)
(Photo: The Butter Information Council)

SOUTH AFRICA

Chicken and Tomato Bredie

Serves 6
Power Level Full
Cooking Time 15 minutes

2 tblsp corn oil
8oz (225g) onions
1 garlic clove
1 small green chilli
8oz (225g) tomatoes, blanched and skinned
1¾lb (750g) boned chicken breasts (weighed after boning)
1 level tsp brown sugar
½ level tblsp tomato purée
1 to 2 level tsp salt

Bredie abounds in South Africa and is simply the common name for a stew. This one is a tasty contribution and goes especially well with rice, cooked carrots and sweetcorn. As it is unthickened, the Bredie can be adopted by dieters and eaten with a green salad or a baked jacket potato without extras – no butter, margarine or cream.

1. Pour corn oil into a 10-inch (25cm) round dish. Peel onions and garlic then finely chop. Halve chilli, remove seeds and chop up green flesh. Add all prepared ingredients to oil in bowl, stir well to mix and cook, uncovered, for 5 minutes.

2. Meanwhile, slice tomatoes then cut washed and dried chicken into small cubes.

3. Add to dish with remaining ingredients, stir well and form into a ring round edges of dish, leaving a slight hollow in the middle.

4. Cover with cling wrap, nick twice and cook 10 minutes. Stand for 5 minutes before serving.

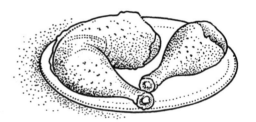

SOUTH AMERICA

Serves 4
Power Level Full
Cooking Time 14 minutes

6oz (175g) onions

10oz (275g) chayote (gourd)

4oz (125g) tomatoes,
blanched and skinned

1lb (450 to 500g) lean beef,
coarsely minced (do this at
home if possible)

2 level tsp salt

Brazilian Chopped Meat

Most countries use minced meat in one way or another and this is a variation from Brazil. Another follows. The usual accompaniments are creamed potatoes or Brazilian rice.

1. Peel onions and finely chop. Peel and cube chayote. Chop up tomatoes. Put all together in an 8-inch (20cm) round dish and mix thoroughly.

2. Cover with cling wrap and nick twice. Cook 10 minutes, turning 3 times. Uncover and stir well to break up the meat. Cover as above and continue to cook a further 4 minutes or until liquid bubbles. Stand 4 minutes, add salt, stir round and serve.

Tips

1. The meat should be of a fairly loose consistency in its unthickened gravy.

2. Marrow may be substituted for chayote. It should weigh the same after peeling and deseeding.

Brazilian Chopped Meat with Egg and Olives

Make as above minus the chayote. Instead, cook meat with 4 tblsp beef stock or water. Stir in wedges of hardboiled eggs and green or black olives at the very end.

Brazilian Rice

See rice – to cook (pages 149–50). To begin with, heat rice with 1 medium chopped onion and 1oz (25g) margarine for 2 minutes, uncovered, at full power. Add 2 skinned and chopped tomatoes and the water. Cover and continue to cook as directed.

SWITZERLAND

Serves 6–8
Power Level Full
Cooking Time 7–8 minutes

8oz (225g) Emmental cheese

1lb (450g) Gruyère cheese

---

1 garlic clove

---

1 level tblsp cornflour

---

*½pt (275ml) German or
Alsation white wine*

---

2 tsp lemon juice

---

*2 tblsp Kirsch (colourless
cherry brandy)*

Salt and pepper to taste

---

*Cubes of crusty French bread
for dipping*

Fondue

The friendly dish where everyone dips in and has
a go – marvellous for parties and, taking into
account the number of people a fondue serves,
comparatively economical. For the true Swiss
version, try to use the cheeses below, and the
Kirsch.

1. Finely grate cheeses into a large bowl. Peel
   garlic and crush on top.

2. Stir in all remaining ingredients except the last
   three. Leave uncovered and cook 7 to 8
   minutes or until cheese mixture bubbles
   gently, stirring 4 times. The cheese should
   also have melted completely.

3. Stand 2 minutes. Stir in Kirsch, season to taste
   with salt and pepper and take to the table.

133

Accompany with long handled forks and bread cubes for dipping into the fondue.

Fondue, Dutch Style

It has been said that the fondue started in Holland where it was called something like cheese dip and made by thrifty farming housewives from left-overs. For a change from Swiss, use all Gouda cheese and substitute Genever (Dutch gin) instead of Kirsch.

Chicken Amandine

Pleasingly sophisticated and elegantly-flavoured, I would recommend this for a small, stylish dinner party. Accompany with brown rice sprinkled with toasted and coarsely chopped cashews, and some cooked broccoli engulfed in lukewarm French dressing. You will need a large dish for manoeuverability and the addition of condensed soup makes for easy preparation.

1. Wash and dry poussin and put into a capacious dish to form a single layer. If need be, choose a deep dish one so that birds can be partially lifted up and rest against sides.

2. Cover with cling wrap, nick twice and cook 25 minutes, turning dish 4 times.

3. Put soup into a bowl. Beat in sherry, garlic and liquid from dish in which poussin were cooking. Pour over poussin (for sauce). Cover with cling wrap, nick twice and continue to cook for a further 15 minutes.

135

4. Transfer poussin to individual plates, coat with sauce and sprinkle each with almonds.

Tip
Heat remaining soup with an equal amount of water and drink the next day. It should serve one.

Serves 4
Power Level Full
Cooking Time 45 to 52 minutes

8oz (225g) long grain brown rice

2oz (50g) wild rice

2pt (1¼ litre) boiling water

2 level tsp salt

2 large spring onions, trimmed to 6 inch (15cm) in length

2-inch (5cm) piece of hot green chilli (fresh)

12oz (350g) blanched and skinned tomatoes

4oz (125g) button mushrooms, wiped clean

8oz (225g) cottage cheese

3oz (75g) cheddar cheese, grated

Country Cottage and Rice Casserole

A spectacular dish and an amalgam of ideas brought back from visits to the Eastern Seaboard and California. It is particularly suitable for vegetarians or those observing Lenten customs and I serve it with a seemingly unlikely condiment – a sauce made by puréeing in a blender 2oz (50g) fresh cardamom leaves with 1 peeled garlic clove, ½-inch (1.25cm) square of fresh chilli then sharpening the mix with 3 tblsp cider vinegar to taste. Also some salt for flavour; about ½ tsp. Believe it or not, the condiment is an Afghan speciality that goes with a kind of meat stew but responds equally well to change and is happy enough with the Casserole.

1. Put brown rice and wild rice into a mixing bowl. Add boiling water and salt. Cover with cling wrap and nick twice. Cook 40 to 45 minutes when the rice should be tender and plump. Remove from oven, drain if necessary and keep on one side.

2. Trim and wash spring onions then cut into ¼-inch (5mm) thick slices. Finely chop chilli then slice tomatoes and mushrooms fairly thinly.

3. Fill a 3pt (1.75 litre) greased casserole dish with alternate layers of rice, cottage cheese, spring onions, tomatoes and mushrooms, sprinkling chopped chilli between layers.

4. Sprinkle thickly with the grated cheese and microwave, uncovered, for 5 to 7 minutes or until well heated through.

Tips

1. Although there is no time saving cooking rice in the microwave, it is more economical on fuel and the kitchen doesn't steam up.

2. Wild rice, available from speciality food shops, is a form of hand picked grass. It is very costly, hence the small amount used in the recipe.

Reuben Sandwich

Serves 1 or 2
Power Level Defrost and Full
Cooking Time 3 minutes

2 slices bread

Mayonnaise

4oz (125g) salt beef, brisket or pastrami, in thinnish slices

6oz (175g) Sauerkraut (drained weight)

3 slices of packeted processed Cheddar cheese

An American dream and a giant of a warm open sandwich which works to perfection in the microwave. It's served all over the US but the best for me from D. B. Kaplan's in Chicago and the famous Carnegie Deli in Manhatten. Make a special journey.

1. Stand slices of bread on a plate, side by side,

to form a single layer. Spread with
mayonnaise. Cook 1½ minutes at defrost.

2. Cover evenly with the beef, spread with
   sauerkraut then top with slices of cheese.

3. Return to oven and microwave for 1½
   minutes at full or until cheese begins to melt.
   Eat warm.

Note of authenticity

Gruyère or Emmental is the traditional cheese,
so use 2oz (50g) grated or in slices.

Reuben Vegger

My adaptation:

Omit beef and substitute sliced hard boiled eggs
(two) or 3 large sliced tomatoes.

Serves 8–10
Power Level Full
**Cooking Time 45 to 55
minutes**

---

*3½lb (1.75kg) pumpkin (½ a
small one is best)*

---

*8oz (225g) shortcrust pastry,
made with 8oz (225g) plain
flour, 4oz (125g) fat and
water to mix*

---

*1 slightly rounded tblsp black
treacle or molasses*

Pumpkin Pie

A must for North American Thanksgiving,
celebrated by every race and creed on the last
Thursday of November, is the Pumpkin Pie,
fragrantly spiced and the colour of a ginger snap.
Too good to miss when the pumpkin season is in
full swing, it is quickly made in the microwave
but I would recommend a food processor or
blender alongside for puréeing the pumpkin.

1. Remove seeds from pumpkin and stand the
   half upside down on a plate. Leave uncovered

6oz (175g) light brown soft sugar

1 level tblsp cornflour

2 level tsp allspice

1 level tsp cinnamon

¼pt (150ml) double cream

3 eggs (Grade 2)

and cook 18 minutes until flesh is soft. Scoop out of skin and leave to cool.

2. Roll out pastry fairly thinly and use to cover base and sides of a 9-inch (23cm) round dish. Prick well all over, leave uncovered and cook 7 minutes. Turn dish 4 times.

3. Purée pumpkin in a blender or food processor until smooth. Spoon into bowl and thoroughly beat in remaining ingredients.

4. Pour into pastry case. Leave uncovered and cook 20 to 30 minutes or until set, turning pie at least 4 times. Eat warm with whipped cream.

Serves 10
Power Level Full
Cooking Time 12½ minutes

Base

3oz (75g) butter

8oz (225g) digestive biscuits, spice or ginger, crushed

2oz (50g) caster sugar

Cheese filling

1½lb (750g) cream cheese (loose from the delicatessen counter, rather than packeted)

Peanut Butter Cheesecake

An idea I picked up at Smollensky's Balloon, an American style restaurant opposite London's Ritz Hotel. Nowhere can one find bigger or better puds and though the recipe remains a secret of its American owner, Mike Gottlieb, I tried to work out one for myself and this is the result.

1. Well grease a 10-inch (25cm) round about 2-inch (10cm) deep dish. Add butter and

139

4oz (125g) chunky peanut butter

4oz (125g) caster sugar

3 eggs (Grade 1)

1 tsp vanilla essence

2 level tblsp cornflour

1 carton (20cl or 7oz) Crème Fraîche

or

¼pt (150ml) double cream

melt, uncovered, for 2½ minutes. Stir in crushed biscuits and sugar. Spread over base of dish and refrigerate until set – about 30 minutes.

2. Warm up cheese and peanut butter to room temperature. Put both into a large bowl and beat until smooth.

3. Beat in all remaining ingredients and pour into dish over biscuit base. Leave uncovered and cook 10 minutes, turning dish 4 times.

4. Leave to stand 10 minutes. Sprinkle top with cinnamon or, for even more richness, spread with carton (5oz or 142ml) soured cream. For near obscenity, cover with 1 can of fruit pie filling, flavour to suit, on top of the cream. It makes a stupendous sweet.

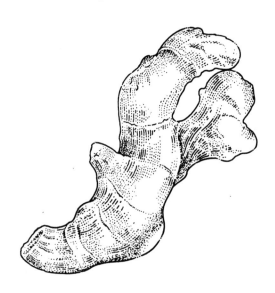

USA-CHINESE

Fast Chicken Chow Mein

Serves 4
Power Level Full
Cooking Time 10 minutes

8oz (225g) cucumber, peeled

10oz (275g) cold cooked chicken

1 pack (about 1lb or 450g) frozen Chow Mein mix, partially thawed

2 tblsp soy sauce

2 tblsp medium sherry

1 tsp sesame oil (for delicious nutty flavour)

½ level tsp salt

Quite good, quite fun, no trouble.

1. Cut cucumber into small cubes and repeat with chicken. Put both into a 3pt (1.75 litre) dish.

2. Stir in Chow Mein mix with rest of ingredients. Cover dish with lid or cling wrap and nick twice.

3. Cook 10 minutes. Stand 2 minutes then serve with rice or noodles.

USA-HAWAII

Serves 6
Power Level Full
Cooking Time 19 minutes

2lb (just under 1kg) lean pork

1 tblsp groundnut oil

4oz (125g) onion

2 garlic cloves

1 level tblsp cornflour

1 can (just over 15oz or 432g) crushed pineapple in own juice

3 tblsp soy sauce

1 level tsp finely minced ginger (from a jar, already prepared or use ground dried ginger

Pineapple and Pork Casserole

Tropical lushness and exotic beauty make the Pacific island of Hawaii one of the most desirable holiday spots in the world and visitors can be assured of a genuine aloha and the gift of a colourful necklace of flowers, called a lei, on arrival. The food reflects the diverse taste of the inhabitants and is an intermingling of East and West with undertones of Oriental cooking in the way fish (always abundant), meat, fruit and vegetables are prepared. This pineapple and pork dish, spiced with soy sauce and ginger, is a typical example of delicacy with fine flavour.

1. Wash and dry pork. Cut into dice-sized pieces.

2. Pour oil into a 9-inch (23cm) round dish. Twirl until the base is well covered.

3. Peel and chop onion finely. Put into dish then

add garlic, first peeled and crushed. Leave uncovered and cook 3 minutes.

4. Stir in cornflour, crushed pineapple with juice, soy sauce, ginger and pork. Arrange in a ring in dish, leaving a small hollow in the centre.

5. Cover with cling wrap, nick twice and cook 16 minutes, turning 3 times. Stand 5 minutes, stir well and serve with rice.

Tip
There should be sufficient salt from the soy sauce. If not, adjust to taste by adding more salt to taste.

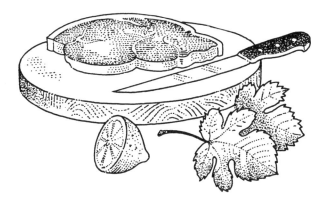

USA-ITALIAN

Serves 4
Power Level Full
Cooking Time 23 minutes

2lb (900 to 1000g) chicken drumsticks, thawed conventionally or in the microwave

---

6oz (175g) onions

2oz (50g) celery

---

1 rounded tblsp mustard with crushed mustard seeds

½ level tsp paprika

---

1 tsp Worcester sauce

---

1 can (about 14oz or 400g) tomatoes in tomato juice

4oz (125g) pastini (any small pasta)

1½ level tsp salt

Southern Chicken in Barbecue Sauce with Pastini

Non-energetic and undemanding, you will find this a useful recipe to have on standby when the only thing left in the freezer is a packet of chicken drumsticks! Additionally, youngsters love it.

1. Wash and dry drumsticks then arrange, like spokes of a wheel, in a large and shallow 10-inch (25cm) dish. Make sure the bony ends face the centre so that fleshy portions are against edge of dish.

2. Cover with cling wrap. Nick twice and cook 8 minutes, turning dish 3 times. Meanwhile, peel onions and finely chop. Repeat with scrubbed celery.

3. Put vegetables into a bowl. Stir in mustard, paprika, Worcester sauce, crushed down

144

tomatoes, pastini and salt. Remove dish of chicken from microwave and carefully pour liquid into tomato mixture.

4. Stir well, spoon over chicken and cover as above. Cook a further 15 minutes, turning dish twice. Serve with peas or a crisp green salad.

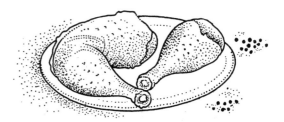

USA-
LOUISIANA

Serves 6
Power Level Defrost and
Full
Cooking Time 28–28½
minutes

1oz (25g) butter or margarine

1½lb (675g) aubergines

1½ level tsp salt

3 tblsp boiling water

4oz (125g) onions

1lb (450 to 500g) lean minced
beef

3oz (75g) fresh brown
breadcrumbs

¼ level tsp Tabasco

2 level tsp salt

Pepper to taste

Aubergine and Beef Casserole

A Southern comfort from the USA bringing
together an unusual mix of tastes and textures as
aubergines are combined with crumbs, Tabasco
and minced beef. The end result is a stylish
casserole, usually served with long grain rice and
a bouffant mixed salad tossed with Thousand
Island dressing.

1. Put butter or margarine in a cup and melt 1 to
   1½ minutes at defrost.

2. Wash, dry and peel aubergines then cube
   flesh. Transfer to a fairly large dish or bowl,
   sprinkle with salt then add boiling water.
   Cover with cling wrap, nick twice and cook
   for 14 minutes at full power.

3. Stand 2 minutes, drain thoroughly and work
   to a smooth purée in a food processor or
   blender goblet. Leave aside temporarily.
   Wash and dry dish.

4. Peel and finely grate onions. Mix with beef, half the crumbs, Tabasco and aubergine purée. Season to taste with salt and pepper. Return to dish. Cover as above and cook for 8 minutes at full power.

5. Sprinkle with rest of crumbs then trickle melted butter or margarine over the top. Leave uncovered and continue to cook for a further 5 minutes at full.

Jambalaya with Chicken

Serves 6
Power Level Full
Cooking Time 28 –33½ minutes

12oz (350g) chicken breast without bone

2oz (50g) butter or margarine

8oz (225g) onions, peeled and chopped

4oz (125g) deseeded red pepper, washed and chopped

4oz (125g) deseeded green pepper, washed and chopped

8oz (225g) celery, well-washed and chopped

2 garlic cloves, peeled and crushed

8oz (225g) easy-cook long grain white rice

1 can (14oz or 200g) tomatoes in tomato juice

Assumed to be a cousin of Spain's Paella, Louisiana's Jambalaya is a warm, friendly and spicy blend based on local staples; rice, peppers, celery and onions. It is a meal by itself and no more trimmings are necessary.

1. Wash and dry chicken and arrange round sides of a 9-inch (23cm) round dish. Cover with cling wrap, nick twice and cook 7 minutes. Stand 2 minutes, transfer chicken to a board and cut into dice.

2. Reserve liquid that cooked out of chicken and pour into a bowl. Wash and dry dish, add butter or margarine and melt about 1 to 1½ minutes.

3. Stir in rest of ingredients and diced chicken, squashing down tomatoes and adding chicken liquid. Cover as above then cook about 20 to

147

25 minutes or until rice grains are dry and have absorbed all the moisture. Stand 5 minutes and serve.

Jambalaya with Ham

Use 12oz (350g) diced cooked ham instead of the chicken, or half and half.

Serves 8
Power Level Full
Cooking Time 34 minutes

2 to 3 level tsp salt
8oz (225g) onions
2 garlic cloves
4oz (125g) celery
4 to 5oz (125 to 150g) green pepper
2oz (50g) unsalted butter
2oz (50g) plain flour
1½pt (900ml) hot vegetable or fish stock
12oz (350g) okra
3 to 4 level tsp salt
2 level tsp ground coriander
1 level tsp turmeric
½ level tsp ground allspice
2 tblsp lemon juice
2 bay leaves
1 to 1½ tsp Tabasco

Prawn Gumbo

From the heart of Louisiana, steaming away in the southern USA, is a unique and traditional dish called Gumbo. It is based on okra and a brown roux with the addition of vegetables, spices, stock and seafood. This soupy stew is generally served in deep bowls, topped with mounds of freshly cooked white rice (pages 149–50).

Many supermarkets are now selling okra (also known as ladies' fingers because of their shape) and it seems to be available all year round from grocery outlets supplying ethnic foods. The vegetable is mucilaginous by nature and therefore an excellent thickening agent.

1. Peel onions, chop finely and put into a bowl. Peel garlic and crush over onions. Wash, scrub and finely chop celery. Wash, de-seed and finely chop pepper. Add both to bowl.

2. Melt butter in a fairly large bowl for 2 minutes. Stir in flour and cook 7 minutes, stirring three times. When ready, the roux should be a warm biscuit colour.

3. Gradually blend in stock and leave aside for

148

1lb (450 to 500g) peeled prawns, thawed if frozen

the moment. To prepare okra, wash and scrub well to remove 'fur' from skin then top and tail. Cut each into 8 pieces.

4. Add to bowl with all remaining ingredients except the last two. Cover with cling wrap and nick twice. Cook 25 minutes. Stand 5 minutes then stir in Tabasco and prawns.

Spoon into warm bowls and add a mound of rice to each. Serve very hot.

Serves 8

Chicken Gumbo
Make as previous recipe but use chicken stock instead of the vegetable stock. After the first 15 minutes of cooking, add 1lb (450g) cooked and cut-up chicken. Re-cover and continue to cook for a further 15 minutes. Stand 5 minutes, stir round and serve.

Chicken to cook
Allow 8 minutes per pound (450g) at full power.

Place washed joints or boned breast in a dish, keeping the centre hollow and placing chicken against edges as far as possible. Season with Worcester sauce, paprika pepper, turmeric and either onion or garlic powder. Avoid salt as it draws out moisture and chicken can become dry. Cook according to weight.

Rice to cook
The method applies to Patna, Basmati and easy-cook American long grain white, or easy-cook brown.

Use 2–3oz (50–75g) of rice per person. Allow a little over double the amount of water to rice; in other words, 4oz (125g) rice to ½pt (275ml) water or 8oz (225g) rice to 1pt (575ml) water.

149

Put rice into a large bowl. Add 1 level tsp salt for 4oz (125g), 2 level for 8oz (225g). Stir in boiling water. Cover bowl with cling wrap and nick twice. Cook 16 to 17 minutes or until grains are dry and no liquid remains. Stand 2 minutes. Fluff up with a fork and serve.

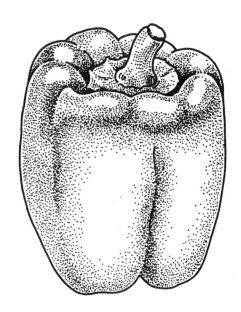

USA-
TEX-MEX

Serves 4
Power Level Full
Cooking Time 15½ minutes

1lb (450–500g) lean minced beef

2oz (50g) onion

4oz (125g) red pepper

Seasoning mix

---

1 to 1½ level tsp salt

---

4 tblsp water

¼ to ½ level tsp cayenne pepper

Topping

---

1 large ripe avocado

Juice ½ lemon

---

3 medium tomatoes

3–4oz (75–125g) Cheddar cheese

Tacos

A hassle-free taste of Mexico, American style. I've speeded things up by using ready made taco seasoning mix and taco shells, taco sauce in a can and freshly minced beef. You can also find the whole thing in a kit – shells, seasoning mix and Taco sauce.

1. Place meat in an 8-inch (20cm) round dish. Spread over base, cover with an inverted plate and cook 6 minutes. Break up meat with a fork.

2. Peel and finely chop onion. Do the same with the de-seeded pepper. Add to beef with packet of seasoning mix, salt, water and cayenne pepper.

3. Stir thoroughly, cover with cling wrap and nick twice. Cook a further 8 minutes, turning 4 times. Stand 5 minutes.

4. Before serving, slit paper once or twice round packet of tacos, stand upright on its base and

151

1 carton 5oz (142ml) sour cream
12 Olives
8 slim spring onions
8 lettuce leaves, shredded

heat 1½ minutes. Fill each one with meat mixture and top with one or a selection of:

sliced avocado sprinkled with lemon juice, slices of tomato, grated Cheddar cheese, soured cream and sliced olives, shredded lettuce, spring onions.

Tostados
Use Tostado shells, which are flat, instead of the Tacos. Put on to plates, pile with cooked meat mixture then use same toppings as for the Tacos.

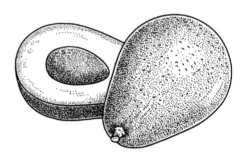

WEST INDIES

Serves 4
Power Level Full
Cooking Time 5 minutes

14oz (400g) plantains

Plantation Plantains

One of my most beloved Penguin paperbacks, *Traditional Jamaica Cookery* by Norma Benghiat, tells of old time plantation dinners, opulent and formal, where plantains were 'de

rigeur' with the cheese course. To revive the past,
I served them a while back to guests with a
perfectly ripened Brie and some soft chèvre
cheese and the combination was an education in
flavours – stunning. Plantains are available from
shops specialising in ethnic foods and are a
relation of the banana, though treated as a
vegetable. Even when ripe they are never eaten
raw but always cooked – there are several ways –
and have the texture of pumpkin and the faint
taste of banana. Plantains also have a pleasing
sweetness and are golden yellow.

1. Wash and dry plantains. Cut in half across the
   middle then cut each half piece lengthwise so
   that flesh is showing.

2. Stand round edge of plate, skin sides down.
   Cover with cling wrap and nick twice.

3. Cook 5 minutes. Stand 2 minutes. Carefully
   remove skin and arrange pieces of plantain on
   a napkin-lined plate.

INDEX

Apple(s)
  Rollmop Salad with 117
  Red Cabbage with 120
Aubergine
  and Beef Casserole 146
  Dip 103
Avgolemono Chicken 65
Avocado
  Chicken and,
  Soup 91

Baby Spinach Gnocchi 92
Bean Sprouts
  Chicken with Vegetables
    and 72
Beans, Green
  Glazed Monkfish with,
    30
Beef
  Aubergine and, Casserole
    146
Berlin Air 49
Biriani, Lamb 77
Boned and Rolled Joints
  without Bone 54
Bortsch 114
  at Speed 115
  Vegetarian 114
Brandy Sauce 58
Brazilian
  Chopped Meat 131
    with Eggs
      and Olives 132
  Rice 132
Bread Sauce 89

Cabbage
  Okra and 14
Red, with Apples 120
Cake(s)
  Cardamom 118

Carrot 88
  Halloween 90
  Honey Nut 69
  Lamingtons 19
  Shearing 61
Cantonese Sea Bass with
  Onions and Ginger 26
Cardamom Cake 118
Carp
  Poached, in Jelly 37
Carrot Cake 88
Casseroles
  Aubergine and Beef 146
  Chicken 111
  Country Cottage and
    Rice 136
  Pineapple and Pork 142
Cauliflower Cheese 50
Celeriac
  Hot, with Hollandaise
    Sauce 35
  Salad 35
Cheese dishes
  Baby Spinach Gnocchi 92
  Cauliflower Cheese 50
  Continental Cheese Cake
    102
  Fondue 133
    Dutch Style 134
  Ham Wrapped Chicory
    in, Sauce 24
  Open Sandwiches with,
    and Salami 73
  Warm Salad of Leaves
    with Goat 48
Cherries in Port Wine Jelly
  55
Chicken
  and Avocado Soup 91
  and Tomato Bredie 129
  Amandine 135

Avgolemono Chicken 65
  Casserole 111
  Fast, Chow Mein 141
  Gumbo 149
  Jambalaya with 147
  Marinaded Chilli 34
  Marinaded, with
    Sweetcorn and Leek 33
  Red-Cooked 31
  Regal, Wings 32
  Roast 87
  Southern, in Barbecue
    Sauce with Pastini 144
  Spiced, with Coconut and
    Coriander 17
  with Eggs 97
  with Vegetables and Bean
    Sprouts 72
Chicory
  Ham Wrapped, in Cheese
    Sauce 24
Chilli
  Marinaded, Chicken 34
Chinese
  Dried Noodles 28
  Fresh Noodles 28
Chocolate
  Hot, Sauce 90
Chopped Egg and Onion
  98
Chow Mein, Fast Chicken
  141
Christmas Pudding 56
Cinnamon Balls for
  Passover 101
Cock-a-Leekie Soup 59
Coconut
  Spiced Chicken with, and
    Coriander 17
Cod
  in Cider Sauce 39

with White Sauce 124
Compôte of Pears in Wine
 with Rum 110
Continental Cheese Cake
 102
Coriander
 Spiced Chicken with
  Coconut and 17
Country Cottage and Rice
 Casserole 136
Crab
 Hot and Sour, Soup 29
Cranberry
 Sauce 118
 Parfait 122
Creamed Potatoes 84

Desserts
 Berlin Air 49
 Brandy Sauce 58
 Cherries in Port Wine
  Jelly 55
 Christmas Pudding 56
 Compôte of Pears in
  Wine with Rum 110
 Continental Cheese Cake
  102
 Cranberry Parfait 122
 Dried Fruit Salad 105
 Kissel 116
 Matzo Balls with Syrup
  100
 Peanut Butter
  Cheesecake 139
 Plantation Plantains 153
 Plum Crumble 58
 Raspberry Coulis 45
 Shredded Dessert with
  Pistachios 104
 Tamarillo Cheesecake
  107
Dolmathes 70
Dried Fruit Salad 105
Duck
 with Orange Sauce 85

Dumpling
 Liver, Soup 21
Dutch Blender Cream 106

Egg(s)
 Brazlian Chopped Meat
  with, and Olives 132
 Chicken with 97
 Chopped, and Onion 98
 Polenta with, and Cream
  112

Farfel/Tarhonya 75
Fast Chicken Chow Mein
 141
Fish dishes
 Cantonese Sea Bass with
  Onions and Ginger 26
 Cod in Cider Sauce 39
 Glazed Monkfish with
  Green Beans 30
 Hot and Sour Crab Soup
  29
 Kippers 51
  potted 52
 Mackerel with Gooseberry
  Sauce 52
 Moules Marinières 44
 Paella 127
 Poached Carp in Jelly 37
 Poached Salmon with
  Hollandaise Sauce 63
 Prawns Madras 81
 Rollmop Salad with
  Apples 117
 Truites en Papillote 43
Fondue 133
 Dutch Style 134
French Style Country Pâté
 40

Ginger
 Cantonese Sea Bass with
  Onions and 26

Glazed Monkfish with
 Green Beans 30
Gooseberry
 Mackerel with, Sauce 52
Greens
 with Vegetables and
  Peanuts 15
Gumbo
 Chicken 149
 Prawn 148

Halloween Cake 90
Ham
 Jambalaya with 148
 Wrapped Chicory in
  Cheese Sauce 24
Hollandaise Sauce
 Poached Salmon with 63
Honey Nut Cake 69
Hot and Sour Crab Soup 29
Hot Celeriac with
 Hollandaise Sauce 35
Hot Chocolate Sauce 90

Jambalaya with Chicken
 147
 with Ham 148

Kidney
 Steak and, Pudding 54
Kippers 51
 Potted 52
Kissel 116
Kneidlech 99
 with Syrup 100
Kohl-rabi Salad 35
Köttbullar 126

Lamb
 Biriani 77
Lamingtons 19
Leek(s)
 Cock-a-Leekie Soup 59
 Marinaded Chicken with
  Sweetcorn and 33

156

Liver
  Dumpling Soup 21
  Pâté 86
    with Orange and
      Pistachios 86

Mackerel
  with Gooseberry Sauce
    52
Madras, Prawns 81
  Vegetable 81
Marinaded Chicken with
  Sweetcorn and Leek 33
Marinaded Chilli Chicken
  34
Matzo Balls 99
  with Syrup 100
Meat dishes
  Aubergine and Beef
    Casserole 146
  Boned and Rolled Joints
    Without Bone 54
  Brazilian Chopped Meat
    131
  Dolmathes 70
  Fast Moussaka 68
  French Style Country
    Pâté 40
  Ham Wrapped Chicory
    in Cheese Sauce 24
  Köttbullar 126
  Lamb Biriani 77
  Moussaka 66
  Pineapple and Pork
    Casserole 142
  Pork Satay 82
  Ragú (Bolognese)
    Sauce 96
  Reuben Sandwich 137
  Roast Leg of Pork with
    Crackling 53
  Steak and Kidney
    Pudding 54
  Tacos 151
Mocha Sauce 88

Monkfish
  Glazed, with Green
    Beans 30
Moules Marinières 44
Moussaka 66
  Fast 68
Mushrooms
  à la Grècque 42
  with Cream 109
Mustard Tomatoes 42

Neapolitan Sauce 94
Niçoise Quiche 47
Noodles
  Chinese Dried 28
  Fresh 28

Okra
  and Cabbage 14
Olives
  Brazilian Chopped Meat
    with Egg and 132
Onion(s)
  Cantonese Sea Bass with,
    and Ginger 26
  Chopped Egg and 98
Open Sandwiches with
    Cheese and Salami 73
Orange
  Duck with, Sauce 85
  Liver Pâtè with, and
    Pistachios 86

Paella 127
Paprika Potatoes 74
Pasta Crema 95
Pâtés
  French Style Country 40
  Liver 86
    with Orange and
      Pistachios 86
Pea, Yellow
  Soup 123
Peanut Butter Cheesecake
  139
Peanuts

Greens with Vegetables
  and 15
Pears
  Compôte of, in Wine
    with Rum 110
Pineapple and Pork
  Casserole 142
Pistachios
  Liver Pâté with Orange
    and 86
  Shredded Dessert with
    104
Plantains, Plantation 153
Plantation Plantains 153
Plum Crumble 58
Poached Carp in Jelly 37
Polenta with Eggs and
  Cream 112
Poppadoms 78
Pork
  Pineapple and, Casserole
    142
  Roast Leg of, With
    Crackling 53
  Satay 82
Potatoes
  Creamed 84
  Paprika 74
Poultry and Game dishes
(see also Chicken)
  Duck with Orange Soup
    85
  Liver Dumpling Soup 21
  Liver Pâté 86
Prawn(s)
  Gumbo 148
  Madras 81
  Quiche 47
Pumpkin Pie 138

Quiche Lorraine 46
  Niçoise 47
  Prawn 47
  Spinach 47
  Tomato 47

Ragú Sauce (Bolognese) 96
Raspberry Coulis 45
Red Cabbage with Apples 120
Red-Cooked Chicken 31
Regal Chicken Wings 32
Reuben Sandwich 137
   Vegger 138
Rice
   Brazilian 132
Roast Chicken 87
   Leg of Pork with Crackling 53
Rollmop Salad with Apples 117

Salad dishes
   Celeriac 35
   Kohl-rabi 35
   Rollmop, with Apples 117
   Warm, of Leaves with Goat Cheese 48

Salami
   Open Sandwiches with Cheese and 73
Salmon
   Poached, with Hollandaise Sauce 63
Satay, Pork 82
Sauces
   Barbecue, Southern Chicken in, with Pastini 144
   Bread 89
   Cider, Cod with 39
   Cranberry 118
   Gooseberry, Mackerel with 52
   Hollandaise, Poached Salmon with 63
   Hot Chocolate 90
   Mocha 88
   Neapolitan 94
   Orange, Duck with 85
   Ragú (Bolognese) 96

Raspberry Coulis 45
Soft Berry Coulis 45
White, Cod with 124
Scotch Broth 60
Sea Bass
   Cantonese, with Onions and Ginger 26
Shearing Cake 61
Shredded Dessert with Pistachios 104
Soft Berry Coulis 45
Soups
   Bortsch 114
     at speed 115
     Vegetarian 115
   Chicken and Avocado 91
   Cock-a-Leekie 59
   Hot and Sour Crab 29
   Liver Dumpling 21
   Scotch Broth 60
   Vegetable Purée 23
   Yellow Pea 123
Southern Chicken in Barbecue Sauce with Pastini 144
Spiced Chicken with Coconut and Coriander 17
Spinach
   Baby, Gnocchi 92
   Quiche 47
Steak and Kidney Pudding 54
Sweetcorn
   Marinaded Chicken with, and Leek 33

Tacos 151
Tamarillo Cheesecake 107
Tarhonya/Farfel 75
Tomato(es)
   Chicken and, Bredie 129
   Mustard 42
   Quiche 47
Tostados 152
Truites en Papillote 43

Vegetables(s)
   Chicken with, and Bean Sprouts 72
   Curry 79
   Greens with, and Peanuts 15
   Madras 81
   Purée Soup 23
Vegetarian dises
   (see also Salad dishes)
   Aubergine Dip 103
   Baby Spinach Gnocchi 92
   Cauliflower Cheese 50
   Chinese Dried and Fresh Noodles 28
   Chopped Egg and Onion 98
   Creamed Potatoes 84
   Country Cottage and Rice Casserole 136
   Greens with Vegetables and Peanuts 15
   Matzo Balls 99
   Mushrooms à la Grècque 42
   Mushrooms with Cream 109
   Mustard Tomatoes 42
   Neapolitan Sauce 94
   Okra and Cabbage 14
   Paprika Tomatoes 74
   Pasta Crema 95
   Polenta with Eggs and Cream 112
   Red Cabbage with Apples 120
   Tarhonya/Farfel 75
   Tomato Quiche 47
   Vegetable Curry 79
   Vegetable Madras 81
   Vegetarian Bortsch 114
   Yellow Pea Soup 123
Warm Salad of Leaves with Goat Cheese 48
Yellow Pea Soup 123